CURRENT LEGAL ESSAYS
Humanitarian & Federal Issues

CURRENT LEGAL ESSAYS

Humanitarian & Federal Issues

N. Sanajaoba

AKANSHA PUBLISHING HOUSE
NEW DELHI - 110 002 (INDIA)

AKANSHA PUBLISHING HOUSE
4649/21-B, Ansari Road
Daryaganj, New Delhi - 110 002
Phones: 23263193, 9811582579
E-mail: ektabooks@yahoo.com

Current Legal Essays

First Published, 2007
ISBN: 978-81-8370-108-2

PRINTED IN INDIA

Published by M.P. Misra for Akansha Publishing House, New Delhi - 110 002 and Printed at Capital Offset Press, Delhi

To

My Mother

IBEMPISHAK

Contents

Acknowledgement *ix*

Preface *xi*

PART I

1. The International Criminal Court 3
   —Elements of Crimes [ICC]
2. Peace and Human Rights in the New World Order 80
3. Human Rights in Armed Conflict Areas 93
4. Revisiting Justice Reddy Report on the Armed Forces Special Powers Act, 1958 104
   —Report of the Committee to Review the AFSPA, 1958

PART II

5. Federalism Issues and Challenges 173
6. Ethnic Conflicts and Resolutions 180
7. Structure of Negotiation between Metropolitan Power & National Liberation Authority 187
   —Belfast Agreement, 1998 [IRA issue]
   —Paris Peace Accord, 1973 [Vietnam war]
   —Oslo II Agreement, 1995[PLO issue]
   —On Greater Homeland demands
8. Early National Institutions [NE region] 228

Annex 240

Index 251

Acknowledgement

The author remains indebted to individuals and fora, which sponsored his following special lectures on critical, federal, ambivalent issues, and national questions of considerable significance in the last and present centuries, which possibly have certain contextual relevance to a couple of the chapters in present book viz., Political Stability in South Asia on 26 June October, 1997, UN & De-Colonisation on 27 June, 1999, East Timor-Autonomy Ballot, 1999 on 4 July, 1999, Minurso's Mandate on Western Sahara on 25 July, 1999, Problem and Prospect of Microstates in 21st century on 1 August, 1999, Non-Self-Governing Territories in the early 21st century on 31 October, 1999, Non-Self-Governing Territories in South Asia on 7 November, 1999, Palestine—From complete eradication to resurrection on 17 January, 2000, Conflict Resolution on Chechenya on 8 August, 2000, Independence Day of East Timor on 20 May, 2002, Montenegro on 8 October, 2006, and Status Plebiscites of Puerto Rico [in the USA] on 22 January, 2007, among a host of other equally significant, analytical talks. Recordings and minutes could have been available with the hosts and organisers.

—NS

Preface

The twenty first century hardly draws a cartographic borderline to celebrate culmination of the agonies of the last century. People rejoice at the imagined emergence of a new world order — euphemistically known as unjust globalization or unipolar world. The capitalist hemisphere has imagined the rosy demise of socialism with the break up of the Soviet Union in 1991 only to witness the Herculean rise of socialist governments in Latin America, and socialist parties in a big show elsewhere.

As happened in the past, hope has never abandoned man in his or her quest for something worth living for. Nation-states could be more interdependent than ever before, yet they have to stay on. The mutual interdependence does not rule out conflicts of national interests, particularly those in armed conflicts. The existing globalization purportedly installs MNCs towards the erosion of sovereign states which cannot be replaced by other entities in the order of the realm. States go to war, conduct business - not the MNCs.

The scourges of the last two world wars might prevent bigger wars, only to be substituted by extensive regional armed conflicts, national liberation wars which did not ripen into their logical conclusion during the high water mark of de-colonisation in the 1960s and 1970s. The political relic survives in South Asia, not excluding the republic of India.

The post-UN world legal order has envisaged a human rights regime everywhere irrespective of cultural, national and ideological barriers of the pre-war past. International humanitarian law has occupied considerable space in nearly all the conflict zones and termination of impunity has been in the agenda of international rule of law, particularly in the international criminal law justicing system. Some states may opt for deviation or aberration, but the world order sets them aside. The establishment and successful functioning of the International Criminal Court — the ICC has overturned the governing principle of impunity of perpetrators of heinous offences for whatever justification that has been made out by the nations or states.

The world public opinion finds optimistic note at the arrest and trial of presidents and prime ministers, who had committed crimes after crime in the name of misconceived nationalism. Nationalism is not dead, but humanity ought not to be punished by the former.

Paradoxically, the world opinion that nodded at the arrest of a Saddam Hussein for killing a few hundred people, also strongly expected that President Bush also be tried for his wilful massacre of several lakhs of innocent Iraqis during his unlawful aggression in independent Iraq for his purported destruction of the absolutely nonexistent WMD in other country, whereas his colossal WMD that could perish itself by computer error or, mistake or powder the world several hundred times over, remains in tact in his own country. ICC can not reach out to some exceptional souls in a few rogue states. ICC, however, sets the rules of the game, and provides for the benchmark of justice. People are not pessimistic for this hole in the international justicing system.

In South Asia, particularly in the post-1950 republic of India, political movements — violent or non-violent, including insurgency occupy the centre stage for half a century. Fundamentalism, terrorism, communal riots, armed conflicts between the state forces and the Non-State Entities or Actors characterize the conflict phenomena. Unresolved federal issues, unaddressed, deeprooted and legitimate national questions that usually happen in multi-national countries might have fermented and catalysed the prolonged, protracted armed struggles of one kind or another. The making of republic of India had been fraught with all the difficulties one could imagine . A solution always follows the problem. Dissolution of problems may take time, yet inevitably it happens.

For historical reasons, the states of the North-Eastern region had been latecomer to the entire Indian nation-building process and even today, problems remain unaddressed to or, insufficiently taken care of by the union government. Draconian laws had been invoked for half a century- however, they appear to be visibly counter-productive. State repression has otherwise spread the prairie fire of discontent to every nook and corner. State repression experts and human rights defenders agree to disagree with each other, and hence, the polemic and social outbursts of huge magnitude.

A rational discourse is naturally inevitable and the small book presents the profile in a small way. Peaceful negotiation conducted by the two parties in the armed conflict — the union government and a guerrilla faction from the erstwhile Naga hills — now, Nagaland state during the last decade could not deliver tangible results whatever and several other potent liberation groups are skeptical about the so called negotiation process.

Demonstration effect eludes the strategy of the powers that be.

Possibly, the structure of negotiation had not been properly constituted from the very inception. In the meantime, irresponsible organized gangs posing as liberation outfits kill and torture unwielding citizens, whereas responsible liberation groups very nearly comply with the international humanitarian norms and principles.

The civil society finds it very difficult to isolate the muddy soil from the sands. Some of the gangs deny basic freedom of the civil society, and gag the media. Fundamentalists of all hues also fish in troubled waters like never before by taking advantage of the federal crisis and legitimate liberation wars, thereby confusing the political outfits and stirring the peace in the civil society. However, common people find themselves confused in the moments of nightmarish crossfire whatever. Human rights, and human security pass through crucial tests in places, where federal crisis have graduated to armed conflicts. The book is a small contribution towards understanding in a small way, certain pertinent issues of the day.

I am thankful to a few individuals and fora, who offered certain space to me — Mr. Alfonso of IAS, Shimla, father V. Thomas of DBYS, Guwahati, Mr. Colin Gonsalves, Prof. S. Shyamkishore and Prof. S. Lokendrajit of Philosophy department of Manipur University, Prof. Ms. Ksh. Bimola, Mr Sharma of All Assam Pensioners' Association, Asom, Mr Sanat K. Chakrabarty, editor of Grassroots Options, Shillong e-pao.net, Imphal and friends as well as media-editors, who had reached out several of my human rights articles including that on AFSPA religiously to human rights defenders, leadership, and the common people in equal measure for quite a long time.

My gratitude also goes to Sri M.P. Misra, proprietor of the Akansha Publishing House, New Delhi for his taking interest in delivering this featherweight idea-package to the knowledge market within a very short time. I have to reluctantly cite the hard work of my daughter Naorem Linthoi, M.Sc., who inspires me from Bangalore city to work at night. I am sure that I have not inspired my daughter. My thanks to my readers and critics too.

Gauhati University,
March, 2007

Professor N. Sanajaoba

PART I

HUMANITARIAN ISSUES

PART I

HUMANITARIAN ISSUES

1

The International Criminal Court: From Impunity to Accountability

POST-NUREMBERG TRIBUNALS

International justicing and international rule of law will never be the same again with the setting up of the first international criminal court in 2002 by the international community at the Hague, following the adoption of the Rome Treaty in 1998. The highest state officials, military echelons, leaders of the rebel groups—the non-state actors and every individual whosoever, who enjoyed for a long time apparent and functional immunity after committing defined heinous crimes would be accountable for individual criminal responsibility in the new international dispensation that would be a revolutionary quantum jump in the history of human justicing comparable in terms of human impact only to the historical emergence of the United Nations in 1945.

The post-world war II mid-twentieth century and the end of cold war in 1990s witnessed not only a political upsurge but also a collateral revolutionary international justicing regime starting from the Nuremberg and Tokyo war crime trials in 1945 to the ongoing UN war crimes tribunals — the ICTY and the ICTR, and henceforth, the ICC (International Criminal Court) in action since 2002, particularly after the arrest of the first ICC subject — Thomas Lubanga Dyilo — leader of the UPC of Congo-Union of Congolese Patriots in 2006. The first page of the ICC trial has opened before the anxious global village, and no one would have to look back. A few powerful countries led by the super power- the USA, which did the midwifery of the ICC and had abandoned the same on irrational and selfish nationalist grounds at the time of delivery keep themselves away from the revolutionary justicing system. The couple of countries may join the international justicing system one fine morning.

The ICC acts in four major states — cases from three sovereign states on their own state referral, and one, on the referral by the UN Security Council to the ICC prosecution. Heinous criminals who got scot free in similar situations in human history are hooked on and booked by the ICC mechanism. Humanity is not looking back to the past characterized by impunity of criminals, that one could never change.

SUDAN: After heinous crimes have been committed at Darfur in Sudan, the UN Security Council by its resolution 1593 (2005) has triggered the prosecution mechanism of the court, the OTP - Office of the Prosecutor had conducted as many as 50 missions to 15 countries, screened 500 witnesses, interviewed witnesses in more than 10 countries and has submitted the 3rd report to the Security Council on the 14 June, 2006. In the midst of armed conflict between Sudan government and Sudan PLA-Peoples Liberation Army, the government failed to stop the sexual violence of women, arbitrary executions and violations of international humanitarian laws and human rights law. The Commission of Enquiry reported the facts on the basis of which the UN Security Council has referred the matter to the ICC -OTP.

CONGO: Following the arrest of Lubango Dyilo by Congolese government with active assistance of French government and MONUC of the UN, the ICC pre-trial chamber held a hearing to inform the accused of the charges labeled against him. If the charges are confirmed, the proper trial would take place in trial chamber. The OTP has opened second case, and is likely to open a third case in Darfur. Jurists, experts and researchers in the West and elsewhere have a field day in the past decade to dissect and analyse the theory and praxis of the ICC. Dyilo has allegedly conscripted children below 15 years in violation of the article 8[2] of the Rome statute, 1998.

UGANDA: On state referral by Uganda, the ICC issued on 14 October, 2005 the first warrant for the arrest of five rebel leaders of the LRA (Lord's Resistance Army) including leader Jospeh Kony and deputy leader Vincent Otti on the charges of their committing war crimes and crimes against humanity like murder, sexual enslavement, attack on civilians, pillaging, rape and conscription of children. The OTP has conducted 16 missions and met 120 GOs. The Uganda government- the military has a truce with the LRA on 29 August, 2006 and has discussed about reaching at a settlement after 20-year armed conflict. However, the ICC arrest warrant stands for investigation and prosecution of the LRA rebel leaders.

CAR: The government of the Central African Republic-CAR- as well as the NSA-Cote d' Ivoire, on a declaration by accepting the ICC jurisdiction, made the reference for prosecution to the OTP on the grounds of commission of war crimes and crimes against humanity by the state forces as a result of armed conflicts between insurgent group, led by the president of the CAR — Francois Bozize on the one hand, and the forces loyal to the former President Ange -Felix Patarse. There had been extrajudicial killings committed by the state security forces, particularly by OCRB (Central Office for the repression of Banditry), kidnappings by the armed groups, denial of fair trial, child labour and torture among others.

The CAR Cour de Cassation also reported that the CAR justicing system is unable to hold effective investigation and prosecution of the accused offenders. The CAR has referred the matter to the ICC on 7 January, 2005 and the OTP has made the assessment of the gravity of the crimes committed and the national jurisdiction before it triggers the mechanisms. The ICC has, however, has not taken up references from Venezuela, as the available information does not form the essential basis for ICC action and also from Iraq, since the situation does not meet the gravity threshold.

SIERRA LEONE: The ICC has not taken action in regard to the Sierra Leone matter; it has rather provided services to the Special Court for Sierra Leone that has been set up by a special agreement between the UN and the Leone government. Charles Taylor, former President of Liberia who assisted the RUF (Revolutionary United Front) of the Sierra Leone which controlled the diamond mine during the 10-year long civil war, has been arrested and to be tried at the Hague following the UN Security Council Resolution 1688(2006) as regards the commission of crimes during the civil war.

CAMBODIA : [UN-Cambodia joint tribunal] After five years of negotiation, the UN and Cambodia government have reached an agreement on 17 March, 2003 to set up a joint tribunal to hold trial of Khmer Rouge leaders, who had committed genocide of 2 million Cambodians during Pol Pot regime (1975-1979). Thirty judges - 17 Cambodians and 13 international judges have been sworn in on July 3, 2006, after modification of the national criminal law in 2004.

Under the amended laws, the former leaders of Democratic Kampuchea would have to be tried for violation of international humanitarian laws (amended art.2), and the suspects would also be tried for committing homicide, torture and religious persecution (amended art. 3). The accused includes aging Khmer Rouge leaders like the Butcher — Ta Mok, among others. The emanating jurisprudence would be an attempt to reconcile the principle of complimentarity with the global concern for international due process. The exercise is experimental though and calls for extensive research.

IRAQ: Iraq war crimes tribunal, approved by the Iraqi Transitional National assembly on August 11, 2005 has been mandated to prosecute and hold trial of high profile top Baath party leaders including His Excellency -the former President Saddam Hussein for committing crime against humanity, war crimes and genocide. The Iraqi tribunal, otherwise known Paul Bremmer court since 2003- the favourite child of a non-existent WMD war of aggression committed by the USA should not have existed at all, as the ICC has the jurisdiction to conduct trial of Saddam Hussein and could have punished him with life imprisonment, as the ICTR did to the Rwandan prime minister. Even under the new dispensation, the Iraqi president has refused to sign a decree of murdering Saddam Hussein — a one time US ally, who later turned out recalcitrant. The international criminal justice has certain flaws that call for attention.

EAST TIMOR: On the other side of Asia, Indonesia which forcibly annexed East Timor in 1975 and caused heinous crimes against the occupied East Timorese people under the pretext of post -annexation Indonesian patriotism, has under international pressure, set up an ad hoc tribunal for East Timor in order to prosecute those who are responsible for committing violence. As the East Timorese government has expressed desire for reconciliation, the possibility of setting up an international tribunal remains conjectural. 2006 UN report covering 2500 pages points out the murder of 1,80,000 East Timorese by the Indonesian occupation force.

UN WAR CRIMES TRIBUNALS—ICTY AND ICTY

The UN Security Council has adopted two statutes in 1993 and 1994, by exercising its powers under chapter VII of the UN charter for the maintenance of peace and security, in former Yugoslavia and Rwanda, and set up for the first time, ICTY—International Criminal Tribunal for the former Yugoslavia and also, the ICTR—the International Criminal Tribunal for Rwanda. The *ratione materiae*, the *ratione personae*, the *ratione loci* and the *ratione temperis* of the two tribunals are well defined.

ICTY: The ICTY has indicted 161 persons so far, found 47 accused guilty including leaders — Ivica Rajic, Martinovic, Nalatilic, Stakic, Nikolic and Jokic for committing grave breaches of Geneva Conventions, violations of laws of war, genocide and crime against humanity. Serbian army had committed heinous crimes in Bosnia, among others, during the break- up process of Yugoslavia. Former President of Yugoslavia Slobodan Milosevic, who had been charged on 66 counts while undergoing trial for five years died in March, 2006. Several cases had been referred to national jurisdiction of Bosnia and Herzegovina as well. Unlike the

ICC jurisdiction, the ICTY and the ICTR jurisdictions get primacy over national jurisdictions, which are otherwise concurrent.

Although the ICTY has concurrent jurisdiction with the national courts, it has primacy over that of the national courts and it may even ask the national jurisdictions to defer its competence in favour of the ICTY.

ICTR: The ICTR on the other hand, has finished 21 trials, and convicted 28 accused for committing crimes of genocide, crimes against humanity and violation of common article 3 of the 4 Geneva Conventions and Protocol II. Several lakhs of Tutsis had been killed by Hutu administration due to intertribal ethnic strife in the civil war in Rwanda. Prime minister his excellency Jean Kambanda had been found guilt, and sentenced to life imprisonment as death penalty is not awarded by the ICTY and ICTR.

An historic decision of the ICTR is cited below not merely for its dramatic value but more of its jurisprudential significance. In 1997 prime minister Jean Kambanda has been arrested and tried by the ICTR. The prime minister has admitted that he controlled the government policy and armed forces at his disposal, mass killings of thousands of Tutsi had been committed by his army in 1994, among others. On 4 September, 1998, ICTR judges- Laity Kama [presiding judge], Lennart Aspegren and Navanethem Pillay have delivered the following verdict:

> "TRIAL CHAMBER I,...
>
> NOTING the Plea of guilty of Jean Kambanda on 1 May 1998 on the Counts of:
>
> COUNT 1: Genocide..., COUNT 2: Conspiracy to commit

> Genocide,... COUNT 3: Direct and public incitement, COUNT 4: Complicity in genocide, ... COUNT 5: Crime against humanity, COUNT 6: Crime against humanity (extermination)... HAVING FOUND Jean Kambanda guilty on all six counts on 1 May 1998
>
> ...
>
> IN PUNISHMENT OF THE ABOVEMENTIONED CRIMES,
>
> SENTENCES Jean Kambanda....
>
> TO LIFE IMPRISONMENT..."
>
> [extract of the verdict -The Prosecutor Vs. Jean Kambanda, Case No. ICTR 97-23-S]

As regards its concurrent jurisdiction with the national courts, the ICTR functions like the ICTY in regard to the national jurisdiction. The ICTY and the ICTR are a class on their own, as they are the judicial organs of the UN, and they paved the way for setting up the ICC in 2002. These tribunals had their predecessors in the Nurenbere and Tokyo tribunals, which are victors' court unlike other UN sponsored tribunals.

Both the ICTY and the ICTR follow the same referral procedure, as the prosecutor has the capacity to initiate investigations *ex officio* or on the baisi of the informations received from UN agencies, governments, IGOs, NGOs and any other sources, unlike the ICC procedures. As regards the ICC, the prosecutor initiates investigations or, the state party or the UN Security Council refers the case to the prosecutor.

The fag end of the twentieth century has brought about revolutionary changes in the international justicing system in the form of the ICTY, the ICTR and the ICC. The jurisprudence they have evolved bears far reaching justicing consequences and enormous legal research inputs had been made even before the adoption of the 1998 Rome Treaty. The third world scholarship lacks behind their western counterparts because largely of illiteracy among the legal elites and university academics; they want to tread the tested and proven paths of research in spite of jumping into the unknown terrain.

The UN diplomatic conference has created the ICC, whereas acting under chapter VII of the UN Charter, the UN Security Council had created the ICTY and the ICTR. The ICC has jurisdiction over the following heinous crimes viz., genocide, crime against humanity and war crimes, as defined by the Rome statute in articles 5 to 8. Under the ICTY statute, the ICTY has jurisdiction over the following offences viz., grave breaches of the 4 Geneva Conventions, 1949, violations of the laws and customs of the war, genocide and crimes against the humanity [Statute articles 2 to 5]. The ICTR statute confines the offences to the following viz., genocide, crimes against humanity, violations of the common article 3 of the four Geneva Conventions, 1949 and of the Additional Protocol, II, 1977. [Statute articles 2 to 4].

The doctrine of individual criminal responsibility that forms the very bedrock and cornerstone of all the tribunals including the ICC has been seeded by the two victor's tribunals in 1945, and this concept emerges as the governing, super-eminent doctrine of contemporary international justice — both revolutionary and popular in this era of human civilization. The only stigma that the two tribunals inherit even to day is that they have been the court of justice of the victors over the vanquished. The ICC bears no such stigma nor disputed political legacy whatever. The IMT set up in 1945 may be examined in retrospect.

Nuremberg Tribunal, set up in 1945 by the statute of the IMT had examined 38,000 defence affidavits signed by 155,000 persons, recorded 703,282,382 mimeo pages, 4000 tones of papers, 2,296,958 photostate pages. It had sentenced 12 important Nazi officials to death including Goering, Ribbentrop, Keitel, Hess, Bormann, and Jodl, among others, for committing crime against peace, crime against humanity and war crimes, particularly in terms of genocide of millions of Jews. Hitler the great fascist and ethnic cleanser of humanity had witnessed ever, missed the opportunity of being tried and executed, as he took his own life in the bunker. Interestingly, during the trial, Goering, defended the greatness of Hitler and Keitel placed every responsibility to his leader Hitler. The tribunal made them individually responsible for the crimes they had committed.

TOKYO TRIBUNAL General Mac Arthur or, otherwise known as Far east or, Tokyo tribunal also sentenced 7 top Japanese officials including Tojo, Kimura and Hirota to death. Sentenced another top 16 Japanese officials to life term for committing crime against Peace and war crimes. Justice R. M. Pal of India had dissented from several of the principles the tribunal had evolved as contrary to then existing international law. The jurisprudence the courts had evolved so far are worthy of intense contemporary, critical scrutiny and research towards evolving the general international law and international justice.

The defence counsel for Germany argued before the International Military Tribunal at Nurenberg that the allied forces deserve trial for commission of war crimes, among others. The victors' tribunal defended that the allies could not be tried for whatever offences they had committed in occupied territories and war crimes they had committed.

Unlike the ICC, the IMT had been totally different. The Tokyo tribunal also defended its stand, "In our opinion the law of the Charter [sic. IMT] is decisive and binding on the Tribunal".

Remarkably, in his dissenting judgement, Indian justice Mr. Pal had laid down the law that the USA had been the aggressor to Japan, and the law of the IMT might not be confined merely to the IMT charter, and it was necessary to go beyond the Charter — the Charter might have been *ultra vires.* He cited authorities like Kelsen and Glueck, among others. The IMT had established the individual criminal responsibility of the Axis authorities, officials and party leaders and individuals, who had committed crimes against peace, crimes against humanity and war crimes. The IMT had, therefore, laid down the jurisprudence of individual criminal responsibility in a different context though.

Humanity has witnessed the scourges of two world wars, the armed conflicts in Yugoslavia, Rwanda, Cambodia, Iraq, East Timor, African countries and elsewhere in Asia or South Asia whatever, and also stood firmly behind the strong emergence of international justicing in the recent past that rendered individuals accountable and individually responsible criminally. This age and civilization can no longer afford to defend the infensible — IMPUNITY, the outdated doctrine, which has surrendered to accountability. The ICC has opened a new page in human history, and it has to prevail upon heinous criminals — presidents, prime ministers, top security officials or, leaders of the NSA [Non-State Actors], whosoever had enjoyed absolute impunity under official patronage or, other forms of immunity for so long a period in human history.

II. INTERNATIONAL CRIMINAL COURT JURISDICTIONAL & ADMISSIBILITY ISSUES

The ICC has started functioning and exercised jurisdiction, considered admissibility matters quite successfully and this hard- won human institution to terminate impunity, fix individual criminal responsibility, promote international due process of law, rule of law and international criminal justicing system has come to stay. By now, ICC fundamentals reach out to the civil society.

The creation of the ICC has been preceded by serious international efforts starting from the exercises made by the International Law Commission during 1949-1954 and subsequently thereafter since 1989 at the initiative of the UN General Assembly. The Statute of the International Criminal Court [ICC] has been adopted on 17 July, 1998 at the UN conference of the Plenipotentiaries of 160 states, 33 IGOs, and 236 NGOs in Rome. The Rome statute came into force in 2002 and the ICC has been inaugurated in March, 2003.

The ICC has started delivering positive results so far. In December 2006, the ICC prosecutor has briefed the UN Security Council about the near completion of the ICC investigations at Darfur in Sudan. In January, 2007, the ICC has confirmed the charges made against Thomas Lubanga Dyilo. The international rule of law has started historical the kick off through the ICC.

The ICC has recorded its success story in 2006. In regard to Uganda, it has issued warrants against 5 members of the LRA- Lord's Resistance Army viz., Joseph Kony, Vincent Otti, Okot Odhiambo, Dominic Ongwen, and Raska Lukwiya, as they had been charged with the commission of crime against humanity and war crimes. The ICC Appeals

Chamber has issued its first decision on merits, on 13 July, 2006 by dismissing prosecutor application for the extraordinary review of a decision delivered by the Pre-Trial Chamber I.

As regards Congo, the prosecutor has opened a second case and prepared possibly for a third case. In 2006, the OTP took up seven situations and dropped the case of Venezuela on the ground of the lack of reasonable basis and that of Iraq on the ground of lack of gravity as required by the threshold of the ICC. It would be difficult to undermine the success story of the ICC within such a brief span of time; it has already evolved its own jurisprudence in the last four years of its successful operation.

The ICC has become an article of faith rather than being considered simply as a deterrence- instrumentality. As the ICC jurisprudence unfolds gradually, certain hiccups call for academic and diplomatic attention. Diplomats, decision- makers, jurists, statesmen and legal researchers demonstrate genuine concern at the interlocking jurisdictional and admissibility issues which the ICC has already experienced. In the following paragraphs, the author does not reiterate the ICC fundamentals, but hastens to focus on the select, profound problem areas and urgent task ahead exclusively.

Ratione Materiae

Drug trafficking and terrorism which could have been included in the concluding negotiation process in Rome may be brought to the ICC material jurisdiction in the near future review conference of the ASP. Unlike international terrorism that had been brought under the regime of a dozen of international conventions, drug trafficking eludes an effective international regime.

Definition of Aggression could be worked out by 2009 as scheduled, with the active efforts of the hyperstates, which apparently are bent upon de-criminalizing the ICC statutory offence in terms of primacy of foreign policy considerations. (see Elements of Crimes appended) .

ICC could remain in seize of the **aggression** issue subsequently after the UN system addresses into the matter. Nurenberg principles and the near consensus so far arrived at, among others' could prepare a better framework. For operational reasons, the opt-out procedure tagged to war crimes could also be tagged to aggression even after aggression has been defined. The opt-out procedure would give breathing states to rogue states and also to inherently aggressive states like the USA.

Ratione Temporis

The ICC statute provides for prospective enforcement of the statute after July 2002 or, after the material state had implemented subsequently after the Rome Treaty ratification. The problem lies in the matter of **Continuous crimes** like enforced disappearances of persons that occurred before the Rome statute had been enforced in a material state — territorial state or state of nationality. The semantic hurdles like 'committed', 'commenced' and 'non-retroactively' would reinforce the ongoing validity of the issue regarding Continuous crimes.

Ratione Personae

The ICC faces the problem of exercising its jurisdiction over certain entities like — the **stateless personnels, dual nationals** and **suspected offenders**. States exercise jurisdiction in customary law over the surrenderees and arguments have been advanced that the ICC would have universal jurisdiction over the surrenderees. Albeit the

US firefighting domestic laws for the Peacekeepers and the existing national jurisdictions over the national components of Peace keeping operations, the UN Security Council reserves its power to make prosecutions either politically or in whatever terms diplomatic nuances would permit. The p-5 enjoys perpetual hegemony over the UN Security Council - the ICC's most potent political trigger mechanism. The USA is virtually the triggering or, otherwise the most cumbersome trigger-perturbing mechanism.

A non-state party can make a declaration by way of accepting the ICC jurisdiction in the matter of **a situation**, and the possibility of aiming the gun at the adversary might not be ruled out. The ICC lacks the authority to ask a state to arrange surrender in regard to third state. On the other hand, the possible abuse by the powers like the USA, of 'Status of Forces Agreement', in order to incapacitate the ICC to reach out to the US personnels is a forseeable issue. The issue of bringing previous offenders under universal jurisdiction is another matter worthy of deeper deliberations relating to impunity termination.

Besides the existence of territories outside the ICC jurisdiction like the High seas, Outer space, Antarctica and other areas unexplored by the comity of nations, question arises about the strict interpretation of article 12 of the 1998 multilateral Treaty. The application of **ratione personae** jurisdiction could be difficult in practical terms, in regard to dissolving states or contested territories and disputed boundarie. 50% of the contemporary international boundaries are apparently disputed. The issue could also be compounded whenever custodial states are involved. Declarations made by some states so as to exclude ICC territorial jurisdiction bears ominous ramifications.

Challenges in the Near Future

The ICC could possibly face certain challenges — apparent and real in its near future operations. The ICC jurisprudence is in the making, and it is the best time for effective legal research, diplomatic attention and moulding positive international concern for mid-path correction or, trajectory re-definition.

The possible challenges could be in the province of sham trials stage-managed by states, lack of extradition treaties or more emphatically in the domain of Amnesty offered by the state or pardon awarded to national offenders, skillfully crafted by states in order to evade the ICC jurisdiction in the thick of cumbersome legalese. The loopholes could be thought about and identified from now on.

Truth commissions established in South Africa or East Timor might have been national political strategies and, at the same time they for extraneous considerations, can reduce accountability to a jargon and resurrect impunity as surrogate deterrence 'Unwillingness' or 'inability' in article 17 of the Rome statute could be easily misconstrued with sham legality.

Well engineered international peace treaties concluded for mutual or unilateral non-prosecution of heinous war criminal as India and Pakistan did in 1971 can comfortably shield forever, the heinous criminals who had committed war crimes and genocide. The **fig leaf peace treaty** could also decorate heinous criminals with the garland of impunity.

Prosecutorial discretion is a two-edged sword; the prosecutor can seek a ruling from the court in matters relating to jurisdictional issues and admissibility. Till the prosecutorial jurisprudence has been firmly determined, moulded and settled, the legalese assault on prosecutor by hyper state are conceivable.

US Doctrine

The USA, which had initially mooted and hammered out the ICC agenda backed out of its own initial agenda. Notwithstanding the pull out at the later stage, the hyper state did not give its signature on the 31st December, 2000 without sharing the ICC philosophy. American foreign policy considerations had probably outweighed the initial US commitments that reached international consensus with sufficient American inputs. The US-created unilateral or bilateral legalese black hole impunity-retention doctrine has twisted the multilateral and consensual ICC operations, which otherwise are pregnant with a brilliant international impunity termination justicing system.

The 'impunity agreements' reached by the state parties to the Rome statute could lead to transgression of state obligations as mooted in article 86 of the statute, and irreparably damage the very foundation of 'international due process of law'. The spirit of article 86 has been left to wilderness in the legalese of the baseless impunity agreements crafted by the hyper state.

The US Black-hole doctrine is preposterous from its first premises that the only super power in the new order would shy away from the multilateral Rome Treaty — its own chosen instrument at the incipient stage, and would attempt to net in the ICC trappings into its bilateral and even unilateral legal event horizon. The US's legalese **assault on articles 12, 15 and 17** of the Rome Treaty on the grounds primarily of the erosion of the absolute national sovereignty and non- party states are found to be baseless, considering the fact that the US-led international human rights regime, its US-led globalization — political, economic and legal agenda, and extradition laws had long back abandoned the insularist unilateralism and medieval absolutist sovereignty. The US public opinion and the law-makers would be able to bring back the powerful super state to the ICC jurisdiction.

The fear psychosis induced by article 12(2) of the Rome statute that haunts the US administration from the very beginning is characterized by the apparent universal jurisdiction the ICC prosecution could seek to apply to the would be American criminals or, forces whatever. International criminal law had long back recognized the universal jurisdiction over international crimes like- piracy, slave trade, terrorism, hijacking, torture, trafficking in child and woman.

The argument that article 12(2) transgresses the treaty law that it should be binding only to contracting parties has overlooked the recent developments in international criminal law, *jus cogens*, international human rights laws, and the justification behind the making of ICTY and ICTR statutes, based upon termination of impunity.

The article 17 complementarity provision is in fact not complementary in the true sense of the term, as it provides a subsidiary ICC forum to the primacy of national and domestic jurisdiction. Looking a little far ahead, in the event of every state party prosecuting and convicting its own homegrown heinous criminals for the commission of the three core crimes of the ICC, article 17 virtually issues a defunct certificate to the ICC mechanism.

The article 98 (Rome Treaty) agreements and instruments reached by the USA government are practically *ultra vires* the Rome treaty. The Armed Personnels'

Protection Act, 2002 (ASPA) — which is otherwise feared by the humanity at large as the **'Hague Invasion Act',** has empowered the US President to shelve US personnels from the ICC jurisdiction, and authorized the President to use force in order to free the US service personnels from the ICC custody in reminiscent of the pre-1991 cold war days. The US government is not worthy of launching international law cold war in the province of contemporary international rule of law, particularly in the ICC province.

The same government has been loudly skeptical of the UN Security Council as an imagined ICC political prosecutor. The USA is the dominant veto-friendly permanent member of the Security Council through which it has materialized its non-negotiable foreign policy objectives. The US-imposed Security Council deferral resolution 1422 of 2002 on condition of annual renewal, has prevented ICC prosecution of UN peacekeeping personnels.

The Security Council resolution 1422 is of questionable legality, and the ICC has its inherent authority to review the illegality of resolution 1422. In the same way as the ICTY has exercised it power to review the legality of the ICTY statute with the active encouragement of the hyper states, the ICC has its inherent power to review the **abuse of Chapter VII** of the UN charter in the context of justicing. The USA could bank upon the same standard in the international criminal law justicing. The resolution has posed a major threat to the ICC jurisdiction and operations.

The ICC has become a hard, irreversible reality and the international community including the hyper states whatsoever has humanitarian obligations to sustain the ICC as the most respectable human institution. The jurisdictional and admissibility issues should, among others, be fully addressed to by the IC, and the ASP as well, in order to remove the teething troubles in the international criminal law justicing system.

FURTHER READING

1. Naorem Sanajaoba, 'The International Criminal Court' in N. Sanajaoba ed, A *Manual of International Humanitarian Law*, Regency, New Delhi, 2004, p 499-; Cf the author's paper on Individual Criminal Responsibility & ICC in the International Seminar on International Law, organized by the ISIL, New Delhi, 2000 proceedings, -see proceedings of one day colloquim on the ICC, 8 September, 2001, Law department, GU, Asom- the author's main address on the ICC and problem, and also his print media publications on the ICC ; see his book- *Meeoibagee haq*, NRC, 1998-ICC p. 186-189.
2. Naorem Sanajaoba, *International Human Rights*, volume I,II,III, Manas, New Delhi, 2005.
3. Naorem Sanajaoba, ICC- Jurisdictional and admissibility Issues, webcast-<www.e-pao.net>, 27 December, 2006.
4. Rome statute of the ICC, 1998 text; Regulations of the Court, ICC, the Hague, 2005.
5. *Elements of Crime*, ICC, the Hague, 2005;
6. Rules of Procedure, ICC, the Hague, 2005;
7. Christopher Keith Hall, The first proposal for a permanent international criminal court. IRRC, No. 322, March 1998, pp. 57-74;
8. Toni Pfanner, The establishment of a permanent international criminal court, IRRC, No. 322, March 1998, pp. 21-28;
9. Marie-Claude Roberge, The new international criminal court: A preliminary assessment, IRRC, N. 325, December, 1998, pp. 671-684;
10. Edoardo Oreppi, The evolution of individual criminal responsibility under International law, IRRC, No. 835. September, 1999, pp. 531-554;
11. Jelena Pejik, Accountability for International crimes, IRRC, No. 845, March 2002, pp. 13-34;
12. Sascha Rolf Luder, The Legal nature of the International Criminal Court and the emergence of supranational elements in international criminal justice, IRRC, No. 845, March 2002, pp. 79-92;

13. Oscar Solera, Complementary jurisdiction and international criminal justice, IRRC. No. 845, March 2002, pp. 145-172;
14. Knut Dormann, Preparatory commission for the International Criminal Court: the elements of war crimes, in IRRC, No. 839, September, 2000, pp. 771-796;
15. Charles Garraway, Suprior Orders and the International Criminal Court: Justice delivered or Justice denied, in IRRC, No. 836, December, 1999, pp. 785-794;
16. Paul Tavernier, The experience of the International Criminal Tribunals for the former Yugoslavia and for Rwanda, IRRC, No. 321, September-December, 1997, pp. 605-622;
17. Payam Akhvan, Beyond Impunity: Can International Criminal Justice Prevent Future Atrocities ?, in the *American Journal of International Law*, vol. 95, No. 1, Jan. 2001, pp. 7-31;
18. Human Rights Watch, The International Criminal Court: How Nongovernmental Organisations Can Contribute to..., September 2004;
19. Robert Kolb, The Jurisprudence of the Yugoslav and Rwandan Criminal Tribunals on their jurisdiction and International Crimes, *The British Yearbook of International Law*, Oxford, 2004, pp. 271-361;
20. Burns H. Weston, Richard A. Falk, et al., International Law and World Order. West Group, 1997, pp. 177-250;
21. Niels Blokker and Sammuller, International Criminal Court, *Hague Yearbook of International Law*, 2002, pp. 173-245;
22. Claire de Than and Edwin Shorts, *International Criminal Law and Human Rights*, Sweet and Maxwell, 2003, pp. 271-341;
23. Speeches from delegates, 17 July, 1998, www.un.org/icc/speeches/717aus.htm
24. Ibid. Final Act of the United Nations Diplomatic conference, 17 July, 1998;
25. Amnesty International, The International Criminal Court, Fact Sheet 6-Ensuring Justice for victims, April, 2005;
26. Johan D. van der Vyver, Personal and Territorial Jurisdiction of the International Criminal Court, *Emory International Law Review*, vol. 14, Spring 2000, Atlanta, pp. 1-103;
27. DapoAkande, International Law Immunities and the International Criminal Court, *American Journal of International Law,* July, 2004 vol. 98. no. 3. pp. 671-684;

28. International Criminal Law and the role of Domestic Courts, editorial comments, *AJIL*, January 2001, vol. 95. No. 1, pp. 120-131;
29. International Criminal Court, Background Information Situation in Democratic: Republic of the Congo, 74th plenary meeting, 20 December, 2004;
30. Hisashi Owada, The Creation of the International Criminal Court—A Critical Analysis, ISII, millennium conference, supra f.n. 1;
31. Yoram Dinstein and Mala Tabory, ed., *War Crimes in International Law,* Martinus Nijhoff Publishers, the Hague,
32. John Alan Appleman, *Military Tribunals and International Crimes*, Bobb Merils, 1954
33. Statement by Phillipe Kirsch, President of the International Criminal Court., 4th session of the Assembly of State Parties, December 2005, the Hague, 28 November, 2005:
34. Report of the Prosecutor of the ICC, Pursuant to UNSCR 1593 (2005)
35. Address by Prosecutor of the ICC, to UNSC<13 December, 2005;
36. Usha Ramanathan, India and the ICC, *Journal of International Criminal Justice*-3, (205) pp. 627-634;
37. Human rights first. The Role of Human Rights NGOs in Relation to ICC Investigations, The Hague, September, 2004;
38. War Crimes- ICC Detainee No.l, McNabb Associates,
39. Jaun Jose Qintana, Violations of international humanitarian law...The international Tribunal for the former Yugoslavia, IRRC, No.300, May-June, 1994, pp. 223-239;
40. William J. Fenriek, The application of the Geneva Conventions by the International Criminal Tribunal for the former Yugoslavia, IRRC, no. 834, June 1994, pp. 671-684;
41. Vhida Nainar and Saumya Uma, Combating Impunity, WRAG, April 2003, Mumbai;
42. M. Cherif Bassiouni ed, *A Treatise on International Criminal Law*, volume I, Crime and Punishment, Charles L. Thomas, Illinois, 1973, pp.1-734;
43. Robert Jennings and Arthur Watts, ed, *Oppenheim's International Law*, 2003;
44. Max Sorensen ed., *A Manual of International Law*, 1968;
45. Malcom N. Shaw, *International Law*, CUP, 1997;

46. Georg Schwarzenberger, *A Manual of International Law*, Professional Books, 1976:
47. J.G. Starke, *Introduction to International Law* 1986, Butterworths,
48. Ian Brownlie, *Principles of Public International Law,* OUP. 1979;
49. D.P.O'Connel, *International Law*, Stevens, volume I and II:
50. Hersch Lauterpacht, *International Law: Collected Papers*, CUP, 1970, volume I, II, II and IV;
51. Ingrid Detter, *The Law of War*, CUP, 2000;
52. ICRC, *Handbook of ICRC,* Geneva, 1994;
53. C.de Rover, *To Serve and to Protect*, ICRC, Geneva, 1998;
54. Knut Dormann, *Elements of War Crimes under the Rome Statute of the International Criminal Court*, CUP, 2003;
55. Mauro Politi and Giuseppe Nesse ed., *The International Criminal Court and the Crime of Aggression. Ashgate,* 2004;
56. Dominic Mc Goldrick, et al. ed., *The Permanent International Criminal Court,* Oxford and Portland Oregon, 2004;.
57. Criminal Law Forum-An International Journal, Rutgers University School of Law, USA vol. 98. No.1 (1994), and other issues;
58. Covey T. Oliver, et al., Cases and Materials on The International Legal System, Westbury, 1995;
59. James Crawford, *The International Law Commission's Articles on State responsibility*, CUP, 2002;
60. Rene Provost, *State Responsibility in International Law,* Ashgate, Datmouth, 2001;
61. Ian Brownlie, *State Responsibility,* Clarendon Press, 200l ;
62. Wayne E. LaFabe, *Modern Criminal Law,* West Publishing Co, 1978;
63. Ilias Bantekas, Susan Nash, *International Criminal Law,* Cavendish Publishing Ltd, 2003;
64. Robert Cryer, *Prosecuting International Crimes,* CUP, 2005;
65. Steven R. Ratner, Jason S. Abrams, *Accountability for Human Rights Atrocities in International Law*, Oxford, 2001;
66. Dominic Mc Goldrick, et al., *The Permanent International Court,* Hart Publishing, North America, 2004;
67. M. Cherif Bassiouni, *International Criminal Law,* Transnational Publishers, NY, 1999:
68. Flavia Lattanzi ed., *The International Criminal Court-*

Comments on the draft Statute, Editoriale Scientifica, 1997;

69. M. Cherif Bassiouni ed., *International Criminal Law,* volume III-Enforcement, Transnational Publisher, NY, 1997;
70. Kraingsak Kittiehaisaree, International Criminal Law, OUP, NY, 2002;
71. Anju Rani, The International Criminal Court and Universal Jurisdiction, *Delhi Law Review*, 2003. xxv;
72. James C. O' Brien, The International Tribunal for violations of International Humanitarian Law in the Former Yugoslavia, *AJIL*, vol. 87, 1903, p. 630-659;
73. Nancy Combs et al., International Courts and Tribunals, *International Lawyer*, vol. 37, 2003, pp. 523-564;
74. Yoram Dinstein, Mala Tabory ed, *War Crimes in International Law,* Martinus Nijhoff Publishers, The Hague, 1996;
75. M. Cherif Bussiouni, Universal Jurisdiction for International Crimes, *Virginia Journal of International Law,* Vol. 42, No. 2, 2002;
76. Willaim W. Burke-White, A Community of Court: Toward a System of International Criminal Law Enforcement, *Michigan Journal of International Law,* No. 1, 2002-3, pp. 1-1001;
77. James Crawford, Execution of Judgements and Foreign Sovereign Immunity, *AJIL*, vol 75, 1981, pp. 671-684;
78. Mohamed El Zeidy, The United States Dropped the Atomic Bomb of Article 16 of the ICC Statute: Security Council Power of Deferrals and Resolution 1422, *Vanderbilt Journal of Transnal Law,* vol 35,2002, No. 5 pp. 15033-1544;
79. Ian Brownlie, *System of the Law of Nations-State Responsibility* Part 1, Clarendon Press, Oxford. 32-164;
80. C.K. Hall, The Third and Fourth Sessions of the UN.... International Criminal Court, *AJIL*, vol. 92. no. 4. October, 1998, pp. 124-1 33 ;
81. Zsu Zsanna Deen-Racsmany, The Nationality of the Offender and the Jurisdiction of the International! Criminal Court, AJIL, vol. 95. 2001, pp 606-623;
82. Robert-Kolb. The Jurisprudence of the Yugoslav and Rwandan Criminal Tribunals. The British Yearbook of International Law, 2000, Oxford Clarendon Press, pp. 671-684;
83. Gerhard Werle, *Principles of International Criminal Law,* T.M.C. Asser Press, the Hague, 2005

Document

ELEMENTS OF CRIMES*

Explanatory Note

The structure of the elements of crimes of genocide, crimes against humanity and war crimes follows the structure of the corresponding provisions of articles 6, 7 and 8 of the Rome Statute. Some paragraphs of those articles of the Role Statute list multiple crimes. In those instances, the elements of crimes appear in separate paragraph which correspond to each of those crimes to facilitate the identification of the respective elements.

General Introduction

1. Pursuant to article 9, the following Elements of Crimes shall assist the Court in the interpretation and application of articles 6, 7 and 8, consistent with the Statute. The provisions of the Statute, including article 21 and the general principles set out in Part 3, are applicable to the Elements of Crimes.
2. As stated in article 30, unless otherwise provided, a person shall be criminally responsible and liable for punishment for a crime within the jurisdiction of the Court only if the material elements are committed with intent and knowledge. Where no reference is made in the Elements of Crimes to a mental element for any particular conduct, consequence or circumstance listed, it is understood that the relevant mental element, i.e., intent, knowledge or both, set out in article 30 applies. Exceptions to the article 30 standard, based on the

*Published with permission of International Criminal Court, The Hague, 2005.

Statute, including applicable law under its relevant provisions, are indicated below.

3. Existence of intent and knowledge can be inferred from relevant facts and circumstances.
4. With respect to mental elements associated with elements involving value judgement, such as those using the terms "inhumane" or "severe", it is not necessary that the perpetrator personally completed a particular value judgement, unless otherwise indicated.
5. Grounds for excluding criminal responsibility or the absence thereof are generally not specified in the elements of crimes listed under each crime.[1]
6. The requirement of "unlawfulness" found in the Statute or in other parts of international law, in particular international humanitarian law, is generally not specified in the elements of crimes.
7. The elements of crimes are generally structured in accordance with the following principles:
   - As the elements of crimes focus on the conduct, consequences and circumstances associated with each crime, they are generally listed in that order;
   - When required, a particular mental element is listed after the affected conduct, consequence or circumstance;
   - Contextual circumstances are listed last.
8. As used in the Elements of Crimes, the term "perpetrator" is neutral as to guilt or innocence. The elements, including the appropriate mental elements, apply, *mutatis mutandis*, to all those whose criminal responsibility may fall under articles 25 and 28 of the Statute.

9. A particular conduct may constitute one or more crimes.

10. The use of short titles for the crimes has no legal effect.

Article 6

Genocide

Introduction

- The term "in the context of" would include the initial acts in an emerging pattern;
- The term "manifest" is an objective qualification;
- Notwithstanding the normal requirement for a mental element provided for in article 30, and recognizing that knowledge of the circumstances will usually be addressed in proving genocidal intent, the appropriate requirement, if any, for a mental element regarding this circumstance will need to be decided by the Court on a case-by-case basis.

Article 6 (a)

Genocide by Killing

Elements

1. The perpetrator killed[2] one or more persons.
2. Such person or persons belonged to a particular national, ethnical, racial or religious group.
3. The perpetrator intended to destroy, in whole or in part, that national, ethnical, racial or religious group, as such.
4. The conduct took place in the context of a manifest pattern of similar conduct directed against that group or was conduct that could itself effect such destruction.

Article6 (b)

Genocide by Causing Serious Bodily or Mental Harm

Elements

1. The perpetrator caused serious bodily or mental harm to one or more persons.[3]
2. Such person or persons belonged to a particular national, ethnical, racial or religious group.
3. The perpetrator intended to destroy, in whole or in part, that national, ethnical, racial or religious group, as such.
4. The conduct took place in the context of a manifest pattern of similar conduct directed against that group or was conduct that could itself effect such destruction.

Article 6 (c)

Genocide by Deliberately Inflicting Conditions of Life Calculated to Bring about Physical Destruction

Elements

1. The perpetrator inflicted certain conditions of life upon one or more persons.
2. Such person or persons belonged to a particular national, ethnical, racial or religious group.
3. The perpetrator intended to destroy, in whole or in part, that national, ethnical, racial or religious group, as such.
4. The conditions of life were calculated to bring about the physical destruction of that group, in whole or in part.[4]
5. The conduct took place in the context of a manifest pattern of similar conduct directed against that group or was conduct that could itself effect such destruction.

Article 6 (d)

Genocide by imposing measures intended to prevent births

Elements

1. The perpetrator imposed certain measures upon one or more persons.
2. Such person or persons belonged to a particular national, ethnical, racial or religious group.
3. The perpetrator intended to destroy, in whole or in part, that national, ethnical, racial or religious group, as such.
4. The measures imposed were intended to prevent births within that group.
5. The conduct took place in the context of a manifest pattern of similar conduct directed against that group or was conduct that could itself effect such destruction.

Article 6 (e)

Genocide by Forcibly Transferring Children

Elements

1. The perpetrator forcibly transferred one or more persons.[5]
2. Such person or persons belonged to a particular national, ethnical, racial or religious group.
3. The perpetrator intended to destroy, in whole or in part, that national, ethnical, racial or religious group, as such.
4. The transfer was from that group to another group.
5. The person or persons were under the age of 18 years.

6. The perpetrator knew, or should have known, that the person or persons were under the age of 18 years.
7. The conduct took place in the context of a manifest pattern of similar conduct directed against that group or was conduct that could itself effect such destruction.

Article 7

Crimes against Humanity

Introduction

1. Since article 7 pertains to international criminal law, its provisions, consistent with article 22, must be strictly construed, taking into account that crimes against humanity as defined in article 7 are among the most serious crimes of concern to the international community as a whole, warrant and entail individual criminal responsibility, and require conduct which is impermissible under generally applicable international law, as recognized by the principal legal systems of the world.
2. The last two Elements for each crime against humanity describe the context in which the conduct must take place. These elements clarify the requisite participation in and knowledge of a widespread or systematic attack against a civilian population. However, the last element should not be interpreted as requiring proof that the perpetrator had knowledge of all characteristics of the attack or the precise details of the plan or policy of the State or organization. In the case of an emerging widespread or systematic attack against a civilian population, the intent clause of the last element

indicates that this mental element is satisfied if the perpetrator intended to further such an attack.

3. "Attack directed against a civilian population" in these context elements is understood to mean a course of conduct involving the multiple commission of acts referred to in article 7, paragraph 1, of the Statute against any civilian population, pursuant to or in furtherance of a State or organizational policy to commit such attack. The acts need not constitute a military attack. It is understood that "policy to commit such attack" requires that the State or organization actively promote or encourage such an attack against a civilian population.[6]

Article 7 (1) (a)

Crime against Humanity of Murder

Elements

1. The perpetrator killed[7] one or more persons.
2. The conduct was committed as part of a widespread or systematic attack directed against a civilian population.
3. The perpetrator knew that the conduct was part of or intended the conduct to be part of a widespread or systematic attack against a civilian population.

Article7 (1) (b)

Crime against Humanity of Extermination

Elements

Article 7 (1) (c)

Crime against Humanity of Enslavement

Elements

1. The perpetrator exercised any or all of the powers

attaching to the right of ownership over one or more persons, such as by purchasing, selling, lending or bartering such a person or persons, or by imposing on them a similar deprivation of liberty.[11]

2. The conduct was committed as part of a widespread or systematic attack directed against a civilian population.
3. The perpetrator knew that the conduct was part of or intended the conduct to be part of a widespread or systematic attack directed against a civilian population.

Article 7 (1) (d)

Crime against Humanity of Deportation or Forcible Transfer of Population

Elements

Article 7 (1) (e)

Crime against Humanity of Imprisonment or Other Severe Deprivation of Physical Liberty

Elements

1. The perpetrator imprisoned one or more persons or otherwise severely deprived one or more persons of physical liberty.
2. The gravity of the conduct was such that it was in violation of fundamental rules of international law.
3. The perpetrator was aware of the factual circumstances that established the gravity of the conduct.
4. The conduct was committed as part of a widespread or systematic attack directed against a civilian population.

5. The perpetrator knew that the conduct was part of or intended the conduct to be part of a widespread or systematic attack directed against a civilian population.

Article 7 (1) (f)

Crime against Humanity of Torture[14]

Elements

Article 7 (1) (g)-1

Crime against humanity of rape

Elements

Article 7 (1) (g)-2

Crime against humanity of sexual slavery[17]

Elements

Article 7 (1) (g)-3

Crime against humanity of enforced prostitution

Elements

Article 7 (1) (g)-4

Crime against humanity of forced pregnancy

Elements

Article 7 (1) (g)-5

Crime against humanity of enforced sterilization

Elements

Article 7 (1) (g)-6

Crime against humanity of sexual violence

Elements

Article 7 (1) (h)

Crime against humanity of persecution

Elements

1. The perpetrator severely deprived, contrary to international law,[21] one or more persons of fundamental rights.
2. The perpetrator targeted such person or persons by reason of the identity of a group or collectivity or targeted the group or collectivity as such.
3. Such targeting was based on political, racial, national, ethnic, cultural, religious, gender as defined in article 7, paragraph 3, of the Statute, or other grounds that are universally recognized as impermissible under international law.
4. The conduct was committed in connection with any act referred to in article 7, paragraph 1, of the Statute or any crime within the jurisdiction of the Court.[22]
5. The conduct was committed as part of a widespread or systematic attack directed against a civilian population.
6. The perpetrator knew that the conduct was part of or intended the conduct to be part of a widespread or systematic attack directed against a civilian population.

Article 7 (1) (i)

Crime against humanity of enforced disappearance of persons[23] [24]

Elements

1. The perpetrator:

(a) Arrested, detained[25] [26] or abducted one or more persons; or

(b) Refused to acknowledge the arrest, detention or abduction, or to give information on the fate or whereabouts of such person or persons.

2. (a) Such arrest, detention or abduction was followed or accompanied by a refusal to acknowledge that deprivation of freedom or to give information on the fate or whereabouts of such person or persons; or

   (b) Such refusal was preceded or accompanied by that deprivation of freedom.

3. The perpetrator was aware that:[27]

   (a) Such arrest, detention or abduction would be followed in the ordinary course of events by a refusal to acknowledge that deprivation of freedom or to give information on the fate or whereabouts of such person or persons;[28] or

   (b) Such refusal was preceded or accompanied by that deprivation of freedom.

4. Such arrest, detention or abduction was carried out by, or with the authorization, support or acquiescence of, a State or a political organization.

5. Such refusal to acknowledge that deprivation of freedom or to give information on the fate or whereabouts of such person or persons was carried out by, or with the authorization or support of, such State or political organization.

6. The perpetrator intended to remove such person or persons from the protection of the law for a prolonged period of time.

7. The conduct was committed as part of a widespread or systematic attack directed against a civilian population.

8. The perpetrator knew that the conduct was part of or intended the conduct to be part of a widespread or systematic attack directed against a civilian population.

Article 7 (1) (j)

Crime against humanity of apartheid

Elements

Article 7 (1) (k)

Crime against humanity of other inhumane acts

Elements

1. The perpetrator inflicted great suffering, or serious injury to body or to mental or physical health, by means of an inhumane act.
2. Such act was of a character similar to any other act referred to in article 7, paragraph 1, of the Statute.[30]
3. The perpetrator was aware of the factual circumstances that established the character of the act.
4. The conduct was committed as part of a widespread or systematic attack directed against a civilian population.
5. The perpetrator knew that the conduct was part of or intended the conduct to be part of a widespread or systematic attack directed against a civilian population.

Article 8

War crimes

Introduction

The elements for war crimes under article 8, paragraph

2 (c) and (e), are subject to the limitations addressed in article 8, paragraph 2 (d) and (f), which are not elements of crimes.

The elements for war crimes under article 8, paragraph 2, of the Statute shall be interpreted within the established framework of the international law of armed conflict including, as appropriate, the international law of armed conflict applicable to armed conflict at sea.

With respect to the last two elements listed for each crime:

- There is no requirement for a legal evaluation by the perpetrator as to the existence of an armed conflict or its character as international or non-international;
- In that context there is no requirement for awareness by the perpetrator of the facts that established the character of the conflict as international or non-international;
- There is only a requirement for the awareness of the factual circumstances that established the existence of an armed conflict that is implicit in the terms "took place in the context of and was associated with".

Article 8 (2) (a)

Article 8 (2) (a) (i)

War crime of wilful killing

Elements

1. The perpetrator killed one or more persons.[31]
2. Such person or persons were protected under one or more of the Geneva Conventions of 1949.

3. The perpetrator was aware of the factual circumstances that established that protected status.[32] [33]
4. The conduct took place in the context of and was associated with an international armed conflict.[34]
5. The perpetrator was aware of factual circumstances that established the existence of an armed conflict.

Article 8 (2) (a) (ii)-1

War crime of torture

Elements[35]

Article 8 (2) (a) (ii)-2

War crime of inhuman treatment

Elements

1. The perpetrator inflicted severe physical or mental pain or suffering upon one or more persons.
2. Such person or persons were protected under one or more of the Geneva Conventions of 1949.
3. The perpetrator was aware of the factual circumstances that established that protected status.
4. The conduct took place in the context of and was associated with an international armed conflict.
5. The perpetrator was aware of factual circumstances that established the existence of an armed conflict.

Article 8 (2) (a) (ii)-3

War crime of biological experiments

Elements

1. The perpetrator subjected one or more persons to a particular biological experiment.
2. The experiment seriously endangered the physical

or mental health or integrity of such person or persons.

3. The intent of the experiment was non-therapeutic and it was neither justified by medical reasons nor carried out in such person's or persons' interest.
4. Such person or persons were protected under one or more of the Geneva Conventions of 1949.
5. The perpetrator was aware of the factual circumstances that established that protected status.
6. The conduct took place in the context of and was associated with an international armed conflict.
7. The perpetrator was aware of factual circumstances that established the existence of an armed conflict.

Article 8 (2) (a) (iii)

War crime of wilfully causing great suffering

Elements

1. The perpetrator caused great physical or mental pain or suffering to, or serious injury to body or health of, one or more persons.
2. Such person or persons were protected under one or more of the Geneva Conventions of 1949.
3. The perpetrator was aware of the factual circumstances that established that protected status.
4. The conduct took place in the context of and was associated with an international armed conflict.
5. The perpetrator was aware of factual circumstances that established the existence of an armed conflict.

Article 8 (2) (a) (iv)

War crime of destruction and appropriation of property

Elements

1. The perpetrator destroyed or appropriated certain property.

2. The destruction or appropriation was not justified by military necessity.
3. The destruction or appropriation was extensive and carried out wantonly.
4. Such property was protected under one or more of the Geneva Conventions of 1949.
5. The perpetrator was aware of the factual circumstances that established that protected status.
6. The conduct took place in the context of and was associated with an international armed conflict.
7. The perpetrator was aware of factual circumstances that established the existence of an armed conflict.

Article 8 (2) (a) (v)

War crime of compelling service in hostile forces

Elements

Article 8 (2) (a) (vi)

War crime of denying a fair trial

Elements

1. The perpetrator deprived one or more persons of a fair and regular trial by denying judicial guarantees as defined, in particular, in the third and the fourth Geneva Conventions of 1949.
2. Such person or persons were protected under one or more of the Geneva Conventions of 1949.
3. The perpetrator was aware of the factual circumstances that established that protected status.
4. The conduct took place in the context of and was associated with an international armed conflict.

5. The perpetrator was aware of factual circumstances that established the existence of an armed conflict.

Article 8 (2) (a) (vii)-1

War crime of unlawful deportation and transfer

Elements

1. The perpetrator deported or transferred one or more persons to another State or to another location.
2. Such person or persons were protected under one or more of the Geneva Conventions of 1949.
3. The perpetrator was aware of the factual circumstances that established that protected status.
4. The conduct took place in the context of and was associated with an international armed conflict.
5. The perpetrator was aware of factual circumstances that established the existence of an armed conflict.

Article 8 (2) (a) (vii)-2

War crime of unlawful confinement

Elements

1. The perpetrator confined or continued to confine one or more persons to a certain location.
2. Such person or persons were protected under one or more of the Geneva Conventions of 1949.
3. The perpetrator was aware of the factual circumstances that established that protected status.
4. The conduct took place in the context of and was associated with an international armed conflict.
5. The perpetrator was aware of factual circumstances that established the existence of an armed conflict.

Article 8 (2) (a) (viii)

War crime of taking hostages

Elements

1. The perpetrator seized, detained or otherwise held hostage one or more persons.
2. The perpetrator threatened to kill, injure or continue to detain such person or persons.
3. The perpetrator intended to compel a State, an international organization, a natural or legal person or a group of persons to act or refrain from acting as an explicit or implicit condition for the safety or the release of such person or persons.
4. Such person or persons were protected under one or more of the Geneva Conventions of 1949.
5. The perpetrator was aware of the factual circumstances that established that protected status.
6. The conduct took place in the context of and was associated with an international armed conflict.
7. The perpetrator was aware of factual circumstances that established the existence of an armed conflict.

Article 8 (2) (b)

Article 8 (2) (b) (i)

War crime of attacking civilians

Elements

Article 8 (2) (b) (ii)

War crime of attacking civilian objects

Elements

1. The perpetrator directed an attack.

2. The object of the attack was civilian objects, that is, objects which are not military objectives.
3. The perpetrator intended such civilian objects to be the object of the attack.
4. The conduct took place in the context of and was associated with an international armed conflict.
5. The perpetrator was aware of factual circumstances that established the existence of an armed conflict.

Article 8 (2) (b) (iii)

War crime of attacking personnel or objects involved in a humanitarian assistance or peacekeeping mission

Elements

Article 8 (2) (b) (iv)

War crime of excessive incidental death, injury, or damage

Elements

1. The perpetrator launched an attack.
2. The attack was such that it would cause incidental death or injury to civilians or damage to civilian objects or widespread, long-term and severe damage to the natural environment and that such death, injury or damage would be of such an extent as to be clearly excessive in relation to the concrete and direct overall military advantage anticipated.[36]
3. The perpetrator knew that the attack would cause incidental death or injury to civilians or damage to civilian objects or widespread, long-term and severe damage to the natural environment and that such death, injury or damage would be of such an extent as to be clearly excessive in relation to the concrete and direct overall military advantage anticipated.[37]

4. The conduct took place in the context of and was associated with an international armed conflict.
5. The perpetrator was aware of factual circumstances that established the existence of an armed conflict.

Article 8 (2) (b) (v)

War crime of attacking undefended places[38]

Elements

1. The perpetrator attacked one or more towns, villages, dwellings or buildings.
2. Such towns, villages, dwellings or buildings were open for unresisted occupation.
3. Such towns, villages, dwellings or buildings did not constitute military objectives.
4. The conduct took place in the context of and was associated with an international armed conflict.
5. The perpetrator was aware of factual circumstances that established the existence of an armed conflict.

Article 8 (2) (b) (vi)

War crime of killing or wounding a person *hors de combat*

Elements

1. The perpetrator killed or injured one or more persons.
2. Such person or persons were *hors de combat*.
3. The perpetrator was aware of the factual circumstances that established this status.
4. The conduct took place in the context of and was associated with an international armed conflict.
5. The perpetrator was aware of factual circumstances that established the existence of an armed conflict.

Article 8 (2) (b) (vii)-1

War crime of improper use of a flag of truce

Elements

Article 8 (2) (b) (vii)-2

War crime of improper use of a flag, insignia or uniform of the hostile party

Elements

1. The perpetrator used a flag, insignia or uniform of the hostile party.
2. The perpetrator made such use in a manner prohibited under the international law of armed conflict while engaged in an attack.
3. The perpetrator knew or should have known of the prohibited nature of such use.[40]
4. The conduct resulted in death or serious personal injury.
5. The perpetrator knew that the conduct could result in death or serious personal injury.
6. The conduct took place in the context of and was associated with an international armed conflict.
7. The perpetrator was aware of factual circumstances that established the existence of an armed conflict.

Article 8 (2) (b) (vii)-3

War crime of improper use of a flag, insignia or uniform of the United Nations

Elements

1. The perpetrator used a flag, insignia or uniform of the United Nations.
2. The perpetrator made such use in a manner prohibited under the international law of armed conflict.

3. The perpetrator knew of the prohibited nature of such use.[41]
4. The conduct resulted in death or serious personal injury.
5. The perpetrator knew that the conduct could result in death or serious personal injury.
6. The conduct took place in the context of and was associated with an international armed conflict.
7. The perpetrator was aware of factual circumstances that established the existence of an armed conflict.

Article 8 (2) (b) (vii)-4

War crime of improper use of the distinctive emblems of the Geneva Conventions

Elements

1. The perpetrator used the distinctive emblems of the Geneva Conventions.
2. The perpetrator made such use for combatant purposes[42] in a manner prohibited under the international law of armed conflict.
3. The perpetrator knew or should have known of the prohibited nature of such use.[43]
4. The conduct resulted in death or serious personal injury.
5. The perpetrator knew that the conduct could result in death or serious personal injury.
6. The conduct took place in the context of and was associated with an international armed conflict.
7. The perpetrator was aware of factual circumstances that established the existence of an armed conflict.

Article 8 (2) (b) (viii)

The transfer, directly or indirectly, by the Occupying Power of parts of its own civilian population into the territory it occupies, or the deportation or transfer of all or parts of the population of the occupied territory within or outside this territory

Elements

1. The perpetrator:
   (a) Transferred,[44] directly or indirectly, parts of its own population into the territory it occupies; or
   (b) Deported or transferred all or parts of the population of the occupied territory within or outside this territory.
2. The conduct took place in the context of and was associated with an international armed conflict.
3. The perpetrator was aware of factual circumstances that established the existence of an armed conflict.

Article 8 (2) (b) (ix)

War crime of attacking protected objects[45]

Elements

1. The perpetrator directed an attack.
2. The object of the attack was one or more buildings dedicated to religion, education, art, science or charitable purposes, historic monuments, hospitals or places where the sick and wounded are collected, which were not military objectives.
3. The perpetrator intended such building or buildings dedicated to religion, education, art, science or charitable purposes, historic monuments, hospitals

or places where the sick and wounded are collected, which were not military objectives, to be the object of the attack.

4. The conduct took place in the context of and was associated with an international armed conflict.
5. The perpetrator was aware of factual circumstances that established the existence of an armed conflict.

Article 8 (2) (b) (x)-1

War crime of mutilation

Elements

Article 8 (2) (b) (x)-2

War crime of medical or scientific experiments

Elements

1. The perpetrator subjected one or more persons to a medical or scientific experiment.
2. The experiment caused death or seriously endangered the physical or mental health or integrity of such person or persons.
3. The conduct was neither justified by the medical, dental or hospital treatment of such person or persons concerned nor carried out in such person's or persons' interest.
4. Such person or persons were in the power of an adverse party.
5. The conduct took place in the context of and was associated with an international armed conflict.
6. The perpetrator was aware of factual circumstances that established the existence of an armed conflict.

Article 8 (2) (b) (xi)

War crime of treacherously killing or wounding

Elements

1. The perpetrator invited the confidence or belief of one or more persons that they were entitled to, or were obliged to accord, protection under rules of international law applicable in armed conflict.
2. The perpetrator intended to betray that confidence or belief.
3. The perpetrator killed or injured such person or persons.
4. The perpetrator made use of that confidence or belief in killing or injuring such person or persons.
5. Such person or persons belonged to an adverse party.
6. The conduct took place in the context of and was associated with an international armed conflict.
7. The perpetrator was aware of factual circumstances that established the existence of an armed conflict.

Article 8 (2) (b) (xii)

War crime of denying quarter

Elements

1. The perpetrator declared or ordered that there shall be no survivors.
2. Such declaration or order was given in order to threaten an adversary or to conduct hostilities on the basis that there shall be no survivors.
3. The perpetrator was in a position of effective command or control over the subordinate forces to which the declaration or order was directed.

4. The conduct took place in the context of and was associated with an international armed conflict.
5. The perpetrator was aware of factual circumstances that established the existence of an armed conflict.

Article 8 (2) (b) (xiii)

War crime of destroying or seizing the enemy's property

Elements

1. The perpetrator destroyed or seized certain property.
2. Such property was property of a hostile party.
3. Such property was protected from that destruction or seizure under the international law of armed conflict.
4. The perpetrator was aware of the factual circumstances that established the status of the property.
5. The destruction or seizure was not justified by military necessity.
6. The conduct took place in the context of and was associated with an international armed conflict.
7. The perpetrator was aware of factual circumstances that established the existence of an armed conflict.

Article 8 (2) (b) (xiv)

War crime of depriving the nationals of the hostile power of rights or actions

Elements

1. The perpetrator effected the abolition, suspension or termination of admissibility in a court of law of certain rights or actions.

2. The abolition, suspension or termination was directed at the nationals of a hostile party.
3. The perpetrator intended the abolition, suspension or termination to be directed at the nationals of a hostile party.
4. The conduct took place in the context of and was associated with an international armed conflict.
5. The perpetrator was aware of factual circumstances that established the existence of an armed conflict.

Article 8 (2) (b) (xv)

War crime of compelling participation in military operations

Elements

1. The perpetrator coerced one or more persons by act or threat to take part in military operations against that person's own country or forces.
2. Such person or persons were nationals of a hostile party.
3. The conduct took place in the context of and was associated with an international armed conflict.
4. The perpetrator was aware of factual circumstances that established the existence of an armed conflict.

Article 8 (2) (b) (xvi)

War crime of pillaging

Elements

1. The perpetrator appropriated certain property.
2. The perpetrator intended to deprive the owner of the property and to appropriate it for private or personal use.[47]

3. The appropriation was without the consent of the owner.
4. The conduct took place in the context of and was associated with an international armed conflict.
5. The perpetrator was aware of factual circumstances that established the existence of an armed conflict.

Article 8 (2) (b) (xvii)

War crime of employing poison or poisoned weapons

Elements

Article 8 (2) (b) (xviii)

War crime of employing prohibited gases, liquids, materials or devices

Elements

1. The perpetrator employed a gas or other analogous substance or device.
2. The gas, substance or device was such that it causes death or serious damage to health in the ordinary course of events, through its asphyxiating or toxic properties.[48]
3. The conduct took place in the context of and was associated with an international armed conflict.
4. The perpetrator was aware of factual circumstances that established the existence of an armed conflict.

Article 8 (2) (b) (xix)

War crime of employing prohibited bullets

Elements

Article 8 (2) (b) (xx)

War crime of employing weapons, projectiles or materials or methods of warfare listed in the Annex to the Statute

Elements

[Elements will have to be drafted once weapons, projectiles or material or methods of warfare have been included in an annex to the Statute.]

Article 8 (2) (b) (xxi)

War crime of outrages upon personal dignity

Elements

1. The perpetrator humiliated, degraded or otherwise violated the dignity of one or more persons.[49]
2. The severity of the humiliation, degradation or other violation was of such degree as to be generally recognized as an outrage upon personal dignity.
3. The conduct took place in the context of and was associated with an international armed conflict.
4. The perpetrator was aware of factual circumstances that established the existence of an armed conflict.

Article 8 (2) (b) (xxii)-1

War crime of rape

Elements

Article 8 (2) (b) (xxii)-2

War crime of sexual slavery[52]

Elements

1. The perpetrator exercised any or all of the powers attaching to the right of ownership over one or more persons, such as by purchasing, selling, lending or bartering such a person or persons, or by imposing on them a similar deprivation of liberty.[53]

2. The perpetrator caused such person or persons to engage in one or more acts of a sexual nature.
3. The conduct took place in the context of and was associated with an international armed conflict.
4. The perpetrator was aware of factual circumstances that established the existence of an armed conflict.

Article 8 (2) (b) (xxii)-3

War crime of enforced prostitution

Elements

Article 8 (2) (b) (xxii)-4

War crime of forced pregnancy

Elements

Article 8 (2) (b) (xxii)-5

War crime of enforced sterilization

Elements

1. The perpetrator deprived one or more persons of biological reproductive capacity.[54]
2. The conduct was neither justified by the medical or hospital treatment of the person or persons concerned nor carried out with their genuine consent.[55]
3. The conduct took place in the context of and was associated with an international armed conflict.
4. The perpetrator was aware of factual circumstances that established the existence of an armed conflict.

Article 8 (2) (b) (xxii)-6

War crime of sexual violence

Elements

1. The perpetrator committed an act of a sexual nature

against one or more persons or caused such person or persons to engage in an act of a sexual nature by force, or by threat of force or coercion, such as that caused by fear of violence, duress, detention, psychological oppression or abuse of power, against such person or persons or another person, or by taking advantage of a coercive environment or such person's or persons' incapacity to give genuine consent.

2. The conduct was of a gravity comparable to that of a grave breach of the Geneva Conventions.
3. The perpetrator was aware of the factual circumstances that established the gravity of the conduct.
4. The conduct took place in the context of and was associated with an international armed conflict.
5. The perpetrator was aware of factual circumstances that established the existence of an armed conflict.

Article 8 (2) (b) (xxiii)

War crime of using protected persons as shields

Elements

1. The perpetrator moved or otherwise took advantage of the location of one or more civilians or other persons protected under the international law of armed conflict.
2. The perpetrator intended to shield a military objective from attack or shield, favour or impede military operations.
3. The conduct took place in the context of and was associated with an international armed conflict.

4. The perpetrator was aware of factual circumstances that established the existence of an armed conflict.

Article 8 (2) (b) (xxiv)

War crime of attacking objects or persons using the distinctive emblems of the Geneva Conventions

Elements

1. The perpetrator attacked one or more persons, buildings, medical units or transports or other objects using, in conformity with international law, a distinctive emblem or other method of identification indicating protection under the Geneva Conventions.
2. The perpetrator intended such persons, buildings, units or transports or other objects so using such identification to be the object of the attack.
3. The conduct took place in the context of and was associated with an international armed conflict.
4. The perpetrator was aware of factual circumstances that established the existence of an armed conflict.

Article 8 (2) (b) (xxv)

War crime of starvation as a method of warfare

Elements

1. The perpetrator deprived civilians of objects indispensable to their survival.
2. The perpetrator intended to starve civilians as a method of warfare.
3. The conduct took place in the context of and was associated with an international armed conflict.
4. The perpetrator was aware of factual circumstances that established the existence of an armed conflict.

Article 8 (2) (b) (xxvi)

War crime of using, conscripting or enlisting children

Elements

1. The perpetrator conscripted or enlisted one or more persons into the national armed forces or used one or more persons to participate actively in hostilities.
2. Such person or persons were under the age of 15 years.
3. The perpetrator knew or should have known that such person or persons were under the age of 15 years.
4. The conduct took place in the context of and was associated with an international armed conflict.
5. The perpetrator was aware of factual circumstances that established the existence of an armed conflict.

Article 8 (2) (c)

Article 8 (2) (c) (i)-1

War crime of murder

Elements

1. The perpetrator killed one or more persons.
2. Such person or persons were either *hors de combat*, or were civilians, medical personnel, or religious personnel[56] taking no active part in the hostilities.
3. The perpetrator was aware of the factual circumstances that established this status.
4. The conduct took place in the context of and was associated with an armed conflict not of an international character.
5. The perpetrator was aware of factual circumstances that established the existence of an armed conflict.

Article 8 (2) (c) (i)-2

War crime of mutilation

Elements

1. The perpetrator subjected one or more persons to mutilation, in particular by permanently disfiguring the person or persons, or by permanently disabling or removing an organ or appendage.
2. The conduct was neither justified by the medical, dental or hospital treatment of the person or persons concerned nor carried out in such person's or persons' interests.
3. Such person or persons were either *hors de combat*, or were civilians, medical personnel or religious personnel taking no active part in the hostilities.
4. The perpetrator was aware of the factual circumstances that established this status.
5. The conduct took place in the context of and was associated with an armed conflict not of an international character.
6. The perpetrator was aware of factual circumstances that established the existence of an armed conflict.

Article 8 (2) (c) (i)-3

War crime of cruel treatment

Elements

1. The perpetrator inflicted severe physical or mental pain or suffering upon one or more persons.
2. Such person or persons were either *hors de combat*, or were civilians, medical personnel, or religious personnel taking no active part in the hostilities.
3. The perpetrator was aware of the factual circumstances that established this status.

4. The conduct took place in the context of and was associated with an armed conflict not of an international character.
5. The perpetrator was aware of factual circumstances that established the existence of an armed conflict.

Article 8 (2) (c) (i)-4

War crime of torture

Elements

1. The perpetrator inflicted severe physical or mental pain or suffering upon one or more persons.
2. The perpetrator inflicted the pain or suffering for such purposes as: obtaining information or a confession, punishment, intimidation or coercion or for any reason based on discrimination of any kind.
3. Such person or persons were either *hors de combat*, or were civilians, medical personnel or religious personnel taking no active part in the hostilities.
4. The perpetrator was aware of the factual circumstances that established this status.
5. The conduct took place in the context of and was associated with an armed conflict not of an international character.
6. The perpetrator was aware of factual circumstances that established the existence of an armed conflict.

Article 8 (2) (c) (ii)

War crime of outrages upon personal dignity

Elements

1. The perpetrator humiliated, degraded or otherwise violated the dignity of one or more persons.[57]

2. The severity of the humiliation, degradation or other violation was of such degree as to be generally recognized as an outrage upon personal dignity.
3. Such person or persons were either *hors de combat*, or were civilians, medical personnel or religious personnel taking no active part in the hostilities.
4. The perpetrator was aware of the factual circumstances that established this status.
5. The conduct took place in the context of and was associated with an armed conflict not of an international character.
6. The perpetrator was aware of factual circumstances that established the existence of an armed conflict.

Article 8 (2) (c) (iii)

War crime of taking hostages

Elements

1. The perpetrator seized, detained or otherwise held hostage one or more persons.
2. The perpetrator threatened to kill, injure or continue to detain such person or persons.
3. The perpetrator intended to compel a State, an international organization, a natural or legal person or a group of persons to act or refrain from acting as an explicit or implicit condition for the safety or the release of such person or persons.
4. Such person or persons were either *hors de combat*, or were civilians, medical personnel or religious personnel taking no active part in the hostilities.
5. The perpetrator was aware of the factual circumstances that established this status.

6. The conduct took place in the context of and was associated with an armed conflict not of an international character.
7. The perpetrator was aware of factual circumstances that established the existence of an armed conflict.

Article 8 (2) (c) (iv)

War crime of sentencing or execution without due process

Elements

1. The perpetrator passed sentence or executed one or more persons.[58]
2. Such person or persons were either *hors de combat*, or were civilians, medical personnel or religious personnel taking no active part in the hostilities.
3. The perpetrator was aware of the factual circumstances that established this status.
4. There was no previous judgement pronounced by a court, or the court that rendered judgement was not "regularly constituted", that is, it did not afford the essential guarantees of independence and impartiality, or the court that rendered judgement did not afford all other judicial guarantees generally recognized as indispensable under international law.[59]
5. The perpetrator was aware of the absence of a previous judgement or of the denial of relevant guarantees and the fact that they are essential or indispensable to a fair trial.
6. The conduct took place in the context of and was associated with an armed conflict not of an international character.

7. The perpetrator was aware of factual circumstances that established the existence of an armed conflict.

Article 8 (2) (e)

Article 8 (2) (e) (i)

War crime of attacking civilians

Elements

1. The perpetrator directed an attack.
2. The object of the attack was a civilian population as such or individual civilians not taking direct part in hostilities.
3. The perpetrator intended the civilian population as such or individual civilians not taking direct part in hostilities to be the object of the attack.
4. The conduct took place in the context of and was associated with an armed conflict not of an international character.
5. The perpetrator was aware of factual circumstances that established the existence of an armed conflict.

Article 8 (2) (e) (ii)

War crime of attacking objects or persons using the distinctive emblems of the Geneva Conventions

Elements

1. The perpetrator attacked one or more persons, buildings, medical units or transports or other objects using, in conformity with international law, a distinctive emblem or other method of identification indicating protection under the Geneva Conventions.
2. The perpetrator intended such persons, buildings, units or transports or other objects so using such identification to be the object of the attack.

3. The conduct took place in the context of and was associated with an armed conflict not of an international character.
4. The perpetrator was aware of factual circumstances that established the existence of an armed conflict.

Article 8 (2) (e) (iii)

War crime of attacking personnel or objects involved in a humanitarian assistance or peacekeeping mission

Elements

Article 8 (2) (e) (iv)

War crime of attacking protected objects[60]

Elements

1. The perpetrator directed an attack.
2. The object of the attack was one or more buildings dedicated to religion, education, art, science or charitable purposes, historic monuments, hospitals or places where the sick and wounded are collected, which were not military objectives.
3. The perpetrator intended such building or buildings dedicated to religion, education, art, science or charitable purposes, historic monuments, hospitals or places where the sick and wounded are collected, which were not military objectives, to be the object of the attack.
4. The conduct took place in the context of and was associated with an armed conflict not of an international character.
5. The perpetrator was aware of factual circumstances that established the existence of an armed conflict.

Article 8 (2) (e) (v)

War crime of pillaging

Elements

1. The perpetrator appropriated certain property.
2. The perpetrator intended to deprive the owner of the property and to appropriate it for private or personal use.[61]
3. The appropriation was without the consent of the owner.
4. The conduct took place in the context of and was associated with an armed conflict not of an international character.
5. The perpetrator was aware of factual circumstances that established the existence of an armed conflict.

Article 8 (2) (e) (vi)-1

War crime of rape

Elements

1. The perpetrator invaded[62] the body of a person by conduct resulting in penetration, however slight, of any part of the body of the victim or of the perpetrator with a sexual organ, or of the anal or genital opening of the victim with any object or any other part of the body.
2. The invasion was committed by force, or by threat of force or coercion, such as that caused by fear of violence, duress, detention, psychological oppression or abuse of power, against such person or another person, or by taking advantage of a coercive environment, or the invasion was committed against a person incapable of giving genuine consent.[63]

3. The conduct took place in the context of and was associated with an armed conflict not of an international character.
4. The perpetrator was aware of factual circumstances that established the existence of an armed conflict.

Article 8 (2) (e) (vi)-2

War crime of sexual slavery[64]

Elements

Article 8 (2) (e) (vi)-3

War crime of enforced prostitution

Elements

1. The perpetrator caused one or more persons to engage in one or more acts of a sexual nature by force, or by threat of force or coercion, such as that caused by fear of violence, duress, detention, psychological oppression or abuse of power, against such person or persons or another person, or by taking advantage of a coercive environment or such person's or persons' incapacity to give genuine consent.
2. The perpetrator or another person obtained or expected to obtain pecuniary or other advantage in exchange for or in connection with the acts of a sexual nature.
3. The conduct took place in the context of and was associated with an armed conflict not of an international character.
4. The perpetrator was aware of factual circumstances that established the existence of an armed conflict.

Article 8 (2) (e) (vi)-4

War crime of forced pregnancy

Elements

1. The perpetrator confined one or more women forcibly made pregnant, with the intent of affecting the ethnic composition of any population or carrying out other grave violations of international law.
2. The conduct took place in the context of and was associated with an armed conflict not of an international character.
3. The perpetrator was aware of factual circumstances that established the existence of an armed conflict.

Article 8 (2) (e) (vi)-5

War crime of enforced sterilization

Elements

1. The perpetrator deprived one or more persons of biological reproductive capacity.[66]
2. The conduct was neither justified by the medical or hospital treatment of the person or persons concerned nor carried out with their genuine consent.[67]
3. The conduct took place in the context of and was associated with an armed conflict not of an international character.
4. The perpetrator was aware of factual circumstances that established the existence of an armed conflict.

Article 8 (2) (e) (vi)-6

War crime of sexual violence

Elements

1. The perpetrator committed an act of a sexual nature

against one or more persons or caused such person or persons to engage in an act of a sexual nature by force, or by threat of force or coercion, such as that caused by fear of violence, duress, detention, psychological oppression or abuse of power, against such person or persons or another person, or by taking advantage of a coercive environment or such person's or persons' incapacity to give genuine consent.

2. The conduct was of a gravity comparable to that of a serious violation of article 3 common to the four Geneva Conventions.
3. The perpetrator was aware of the factual circumstances that established the gravity of the conduct.
4. The conduct took place in the context of and was associated with an armed conflict not of an international character.
5. The perpetrator was aware of factual circumstances that established the existence of an armed conflict.

Article 8 (2) (e) (vii)

War crime of using, conscripting and enlisting children

Elements

Article 8 (2) (e) (viii)

War crime of displacing civilians

Elements

1. The perpetrator ordered a displacement of a civilian population.
2. Such order was not justified by the security of the civilians involved or by military necessity.

3. The perpetrator was in a position to effect such displacement by giving such order.
4. The conduct took place in the context of and was associated with an armed conflict not of an international character.
5. The perpetrator was aware of factual circumstances that established the existence of an armed conflict.

Article 8 (2) (e) (ix)

War crime of treacherously killing or wounding

Elements

1. The perpetrator invited the confidence or belief of one or more combatant adversaries that they were entitled to, or were obliged to accord, protection under rules of international law applicable in armed conflict.
2. The perpetrator intended to betray that confidence or belief.
3. The perpetrator killed or injured such person or persons.
4. The perpetrator made use of that confidence or belief in killing or injuring such person or persons.
5. Such person or persons belonged to an adverse party.
6. The conduct took place in the context of and was associated with an armed conflict not of an international character.
7. The perpetrator was aware of factual circumstances that established the existence of an armed conflict.

Article 8 (2) (e) (x)

War crime of denying quarter

Elements

1. The perpetrator declared or ordered that there shall be no survivors.
2. Such declaration or order was given in order to threaten an adversary or to conduct hostilities on the basis that there shall be no survivors.
3. The perpetrator was in a position of effective command or control over the subordinate forces to which the declaration or order was directed.
4. The conduct took place in the context of and was associated with an armed conflict not of an international character.
5. The perpetrator was aware of factual circumstances that established the existence of an armed conflict.

Article8 (2) (e) (xi)-1

War crime of mutilation

Elements

1. The perpetrator subjected one or more persons to mutilation, in particular by permanently disfiguring the person or persons, or by permanently disabling or removing an organ or appendage.
2. The conduct caused death or seriously endangered the physical or mental health of such person or persons.
3. The conduct was neither justified by the medical, dental or hospital treatment of the person or persons concerned nor carried out in such person's or persons' interest.[68]

4. Such person or persons were in the power of another party to the conflict.
5. The conduct took place in the context of and was associated with an armed conflict not of an international character.
6. The perpetrator was aware of factual circumstances that established the existence of an armed conflict.

Article 8 (2) (e) (xi)-2

War crime of medical or scientific experiments

Elements

1. The perpetrator subjected one or more persons to a medical or scientific experiment.
2. The experiment caused the death or seriously endangered the physical or mental health or integrity of such person or persons.
3. The conduct was neither justified by the medical, dental or hospital treatment of such person or persons concerned nor carried out in such person's or persons' interest.
4. Such person or persons were in the power of another party to the conflict.
5. The conduct took place in the context of and was associated with an armed conflict not of an international character.
6. The perpetrator was aware of factual circumstances that established the existence of an armed conflict.

Article 8 (2) (e) (xii)

War crime of destroying or seizing the enemy's property

Elements

1. The perpetrator destroyed or seized certain property.

2. Such property was property of an adversary.
3. Such property was protected from that destruction or seizure under the international law of armed conflict.
4. The perpetrator was aware of the factual circumstances that established the status of the property.
5. The destruction or seizure was not required by military necessity.
6. The conduct took place in the context of and was associated with an armed conflict not of an international character.
7. The perpetrator was aware of factual circumstances that established the existence of an armed conflict.

NOTES

1. This paragraph is without prejudice to the obligation of the Prosecutor under article 54, paragraph 1, of the Statute.
2. The term "killed" is interchangeable with the term "caused death".
3. This conduct may include, but is not necessarily restricted to, acts of torture, rape, sexual violence or inhuman or degrading treatment.
4. The term "conditions of life" may include, but is not necessarily restricted to, deliberate deprivation of resources indispensable for survival, such as food or medical services, or systematic expulsion from homes.
5. The term "forcibly" is not restricted to physical force, but may include threat of force or coercion, such as that caused by fear of violence, duress, detention, psychological oppression or abuse of power, against such person or persons or another person, or by taking advantage of a coercive environment.
6. A policy which has a civilian population as the object of the attack would be implemented by State or organizational action. Such a policy may, in exceptional circumstances, be

implemented by a deliberate failure to take action, which is consciously aimed at encouraging such attack. The existence of such a policy cannot be inferred solely from the absence of governmental or organizational action.

7. The term "killed" is interchangeable with the term "caused death". This footnote applies to all elements which use either of these concepts.
8. The conduct could be committed by different methods of killing, either directly or indirectly.
9. The infliction of such conditions could include the deprivation of access to food and medicine.
10. The term "as part of" would include the initial conduct in a mass killing.
11. It is understood that such deprivation of liberty may, in some circumstances, include exacting forced labour or otherwise reducing a person to a servile status as defined in the Supplementary Convention on the Abolition of Slavery, the Slave Trade, and Institutions and Practices Similar to Slavery of 1956. It is also understood that the conduct described in this element includes trafficking in persons, in particular women and children.
12. The term "forcibly" is not restricted to physical force, but may include threat of force or coercion, such as that caused by fear of violence, duress, detention, psychological oppression or abuse of power against such person or persons or another person, or by taking advantage of a coercive environment.
13. "Deported or forcibly transferred" is interchangeable with "forcibly displaced".
14. It is understood that no specific purpose need be proved for this crime.
15. The concept of "invasion" is intended to be broad enough to be gender-neutral.
16. It is understood that a person may be incapable of giving genuine consent if affected by natural, induced or age-related incapacity. This footnote also applies to the corresponding elements of article 7 (1) (g)-3, 5 and 6.
17. Given the complex nature of this crime, it is recognized that its commission could involve more than one perpetrator as a part of a common criminal purpose.

18. It is understood that such deprivation of liberty may, in some circumstances, include exacting forced labour or otherwise reducing a person to a servile status as defined in the Supplementary Convention on the Abolition of Slavery, the Slave Trade, and Institutions and Practices Similar to Slavery of 1956. It is also understood that the conduct described in this element includes trafficking in persons, in particular women and children.
19. The deprivation is not intended to include birth-control measures which have a non-permanent effect in practice.
20. It is understood that "genuine consent" does not include consent obtained through deception.
21. This requirement is without prejudice to paragraph 6 of the General Introduction to the Elements of Crimes.
22. It is understood that no additional mental element is necessary for this element other than that inherent in element 6.
23. Given the complex nature of this crime, it is recognized that its commission will normally involve more than one perpetrator as a part of a common criminal purpose.
24. This crime falls under the jurisdiction of the Court only if the attack referred to in elements 7 and 8 occurs after the entry into force of the Statute.
25. The word "detained" would include a perpetrator who maintained an existing detention.
26. It is understood that under certain circumstances an arrest or detention may have been lawful.
27. This element, inserted because of the complexity of this crime, is without prejudice to the General Introduction to the Elements of Crimes.
28. It is understood that, in the case of a perpetrator who maintained an existing detention, this element would be satisfied if the perpetrator was aware that such a refusal had already taken place.
29. It is understood that "character" refers to the nature and gravity of the act.
30. It is understood that "character" refers to the nature and gravity of the act.
31. The term "killed" is interchangeable with the term "caused death". This footnote applies to all elements which use either of these concepts.

32. This mental element recognizes the interplay between articles 30 and 32. This footnote also applies to the corresponding element in each crime under article 8 (2) (a), and to the element in other crimes in article 8 (2) concerning the awareness of factual circumstances that establish the status of persons or property protected under the relevant international law of armed conflict.
33. With respect to nationality, it is understood that the perpetrator needs only to know that the victim belonged to an adverse party to the conflict. This footnote also applies to the corresponding element in each crime under article 8 (2) (a).
34. The term "international armed conflict" includes military occupation. This footnote also applies to the corresponding element in each crime under article 8 (2) (a).
35. As element 3 requires that all victims must be "protected persons" under one or more of the Geneva Conventions of 1949, these elements do not include the custody or control requirement found in the elements of article 7 (1) (e).
36. The expression "concrete and direct overall military advantage" refers to a military advantage that is foreseeable by the perpetrator at the relevant time. Such advantage may or may not be temporally or geographically related to the object of the attack. The fact that this crime admits the possibility of lawful incidental injury and collateral damage does not in any way justify any violation of the law applicable in armed conflict. It does not address justifications for war or other rules related to *jus ad bellum*. It reflects the proportionality requirement inherent in determining the legality of any military activity undertaken in the context of an armed conflict.
37. As opposed to the general rule set forth in paragraph 4 of the General Introduction, this knowledge element requires that the perpetrator make the value judgement as described therein. An evaluation of that value judgement must be based on the requisite information available to the perpetrator at the time.
38. The presence in the locality of persons specially protected under the Geneva Conventions of 1949 or of police forces retained for the sole purpose of maintaining law and order does not by itself render the locality a military objective.

39. This mental element recognizes the interplay between article 30 and article 32. The term "prohibited nature" denotes illegality.
40. This mental element recognizes the interplay between article 30 and article 32. The term "prohibited nature" denotes illegality.
41. This mental element recognizes the interplay between article 30 and article 32. The "should have known" test required in the other offences found in article 8 (2) (b) (vii) is not applicable here because of the variable and regulatory nature of the relevant prohibitions.
42. "Combatant purposes" in these circumstances means purposes directly related to hostilities and not including medical, religious or similar activities.
43. This mental element recognizes the interplay between article 30 and article 32. The term "prohibited nature" denotes illegality.
44. The term "transfer" needs to be interpreted in accordance with the relevant provisions of international humanitarian law.
45. The presence in the locality of persons specially protected under the Geneva Conventions of 1949 or of police forces retained for the sole purpose of maintaining law and order does not by itself render the locality a military objective.
46. Consent is not a defence to this crime. The crime prohibits any medical procedure which is not indicated by the state of health of the person concerned and which is not consistent with generally accepted medical standards which would be applied under similar medical circumstances to persons who are nationals of the party conducting the procedure and who are in no way deprived of liberty. This footnote also applies to the same element for article 8 (2) (b) (x) 2.
47. As indicated by the use of the term "private or personal use", appropriations justified by military necessity cannot constitute the crime of pillaging.
48. Nothing in this element shall be interpreted as limiting or prejudicing in any way existing or developing rules of international law with respect to the development, production, stockpiling and use of chemical weapons.

49. For this crime, "persons" can include dead persons. It is understood that the victim need not personally be aware of the existence of the humiliation or degradation or other violation. This element takes into account relevant aspects of the cultural background of the victim.
50. The concept of "invasion" is intended to be broad enough to be gender-neutral.
51. It is understood that a person may be incapable of giving genuine consent if affected by natural, induced or age-related incapacity. This footnote also applies to the corresponding elements of article 8 (2) (b) (xxii)-3, 5 and 6.
52. Given the complex nature of this crime, it is recognized that its commission could involve more than one perpetrator as a part of a common criminal purpose.
53. It is understood that such deprivation of liberty may, in some circumstances, include exacting forced labour or otherwise reducing a person to servile status as defined in the Supplementary Convention on the Abolition of Slavery, the Slave Trade, and Institutions and Practices Similar to Slavery of 1956. It is also understood that the conduct described in this element includes trafficking in persons, in particular women and children.
54. The deprivation is not intended to include birth-control measures which have a non-permanent effect in practice.
55. It is understood that "genuine consent" does not include consent obtained through deception.
56. The term "religious personnel" includes those non-confessional non-combatant military personnel carrying out a similar function.
57. For this crime, "persons" can include dead persons. It is understood that the victim need not personally be aware of the existence of the humiliation or degradation or other violation. This element takes into account relevant aspects of the cultural background of the victim.
58. The elements laid down in these documents do not address the different forms of individual criminal responsibility, as enunciated in articles 25 and 28 of the Statute.
59. With respect to elements 4 and 5, the Court should consider whether, in the light of all relevant circumstances, the

cumulative effect of factors with respect to guarantees deprived the person or persons of a fair trial.

60. The presence in the locality of persons specially protected under the Geneva Conventions of 1949 or of police forces retained for the sole purpose of maintaining law and order does not by itself render the locality a military objective.

61. As indicated by the use of the term "private or personal use", appropriations justified by military necessity cannot constitute the crime of pillaging.

62. The concept of "invasion" is intended to be broad enough to be gender-neutral.

63. It is understood that a person may be incapable of giving genuine consent if affected by natural, induced or age-related incapacity. This footnote also applies to the corresponding elements in article 8 (2) (e) (vi)-3, 5 and 6.

64. Given the complex nature of this crime, it is recognized that its commission could involve more than one perpetrator as a part of a common criminal purpose.

65. It is understood that such deprivation of liberty may, in some circumstances, include exacting forced labour or otherwise reducing a person to servile status as defined in the Supplementary Convention on the Abolition of Slavery, the Slave Trade, and Institutions and Practices Similar to Slavery of 1956. It is also understood that the conduct described in this element includes trafficking in persons, in particular women and children.

66. The deprivation is not intended to include birth-control measures which have a non-permanent effect in practice.

67. It is understood that "genuine consent" does not include consent obtained through deception.

68. Consent is not a defence to this crime. The crime prohibits any medical procedure which is not indicated by the state of health of the person concerned and which is not consistent with generally accepted medical standards which would be applied under similar medical circumstances to persons who are nationals of the party conducting the procedure and who are in no way deprived of liberty. This footnote also applies to the similar element in article 8 (2) (e) (xi)-2.

2

Peace and Human Rights in the New World Order

Peace Initiative is welcome in the regional agenda. In the university campus, when everybody is talking about peace, I was also just thinking about peace.

Hitler has asked his intelligence chief if the Jews were peaceful in Germany and the rest of the world. Intelligence chief of Hitler — the Nazi leader said that yes, all the Jews—about 60 lakh Jews are peaceful now. We have converted them into ashes. Jews will no longer be able to shout now they are peaceful. This is the first meaning of peace. Secondly, when Hitler restored peace in Germany by making 60 lakh Jews into powder, then Stalin, Churchill, and Roosevelt — the three great allied leaders would ask their intelligence chiefs if Germany was peaceful. The intelligence chiefs said that there are no longer houses, buildings, no Germans in Germany, only allied troops are there. Yes, Germany is peaceful now.

The meaning of peace is very easy to find out but peace is the most abused word throughout the world. You commit crime, and you say peace is there. You subjugate people and you say that is peaceful. Armies take a free hand with the citizens, and they call it peace. Even leaders of liberation wars take liberties with the citizens of various sections, and they call it peace. Peace will definitely run away from this world if these statements carry the real meaning of peace.

The structure — the system itself — contains violence. The structure of exploitation, the structure of racism, casteism, the structure of inequality, the structure of deprivation and denial; the structure itself is violent and the response is counter-violence. Whatever we see from outside is totally untrue. Our political senses and the sensibilities are terminated by the massive propaganda mischief. They have given a wrong interpretation of peace. We are for genuine peace. What are the building blocks of peace, what are the foundations of peace and human rights i.e. the agenda we are looking for 7 Regarding North-Eastern states, the North-eastern states have been a distinctive historical entity.

Probably, I will make no exaggeration when I say that Assam had been annexed by British India in 1826. Tripura and Manipur had been taken over by the dominion of India in 1949. The Khasi and Jaintia hills remained independent. Naga hills and the Tuensang areas remained independent. NEFA had been an excluded area. So history -the genuine history — tells that if we read into the archaeology, the pre-history, medieval history, the 19th and the 20th century history, linguistics, anthropology, geography and the people's chemistry, the north-east has remained as a distinct entity.

When we are looking for the true meaning of peace and human rights, we reflect into the past. The past is irreversible. The present is the time for activity and foundation. We can create the future. But without a past and a present, a future does not evolve on its own. In this situation, the meaning of peace and human rights should not be vulgarized. It should not be simplified by what the mass media wants to make us understand in their own way. Mass media is not the only conscience keeper of the society and humanity. Sometimes, they do and often they fail to serve as the conscience of humanity.

Regarding the North-eastern states' relationship with the rest of the world, we are a part of the world definitely, and we would like to be very good players in the game — the world of economics, the world of science, the world of technology, the world of politics and a world where everybody could be free and active. It is the dream of every north-easterner, and if that dream could be fulfilled without taking resort to violence committed by the constitution and the violence committed by the social system, that is the best step that could be taken.

In this global initiative especially after September 11, when the pride of the United States had been brought down by a few youths, they didn't use any bombs, any pistol but they used some kitchen knives, and with one or two secret knives they broke down the ego, the arrogance of the mightiest power of the planet earth — the United States. Thank God, their knives did not touch the White House. From then on, the world has been very much engaged with the new world order--the world that should be free from terrorism. That situation and that September 11 has been taken as the justification by the United States to invade the independent and the sovereign countries. The falsified reasoning is known as the weapons of mass destruction, which they cannot find even today.

If this principle — the President and the Prime Minister whoever are not desirable for America's vital interest have to be a victim of America's arrogance is to be applied then, India may not be an exception. Someday or other, when India or China or Asian countries may not fulfill all the requirements of American interest, they may try to change Manmohan or Sonia Gandhi or Vajpayee, they may still resort to bombing. I don't think that there is international morality in disturbing independent countries.

So, the world order has became a 'disorder'. In understanding that, among scholars in this world, Fukuyama said that it is the end of the history that liberalism will prevail; Samuel Huntington's book "Clash of Civilization" — himself an advisor to the American administration for decades observes that west has a war with Islam and Bush follows this knowingly or unknowingly. America is an exceptionalism in Henry Kissinger's words; then what about Indian exceptionalism, European exceptionalism.

There are the war mongering agenda of the so-called peaceful and peace loving countries. As the problem is that America never wants war on the American soil --be it First World War, Second World War, or possibly the Third World War — America would never arrange a war on the American soil. They will make war on European or Asian soil. This is American exceptionalism, and not the exceptionalism which Henry Kissinger — the Harvard University professor has been preaching through his 'Diplomacy' and many other seminal works.

America has exiled war from American soil, imported war in European, Asian and African soil. I don't think this is the meaning of peace and human rights. The world order after September 11, America-led invasion in Iraq is not an equitable world order, but it is rather a disorder. I may not be the one but there are many good American philosophers and political analysts like Noam Chomsky etc., as in many of his lectures, writings and statements, he says that America is an empire. There are brave people within the soil of America who can understand the original sin of their misconceived and the misinterpreted patriotism. In this situation, how far the global order could give us guidance to the north-eastern states? Multi-lateralism — all the powers of the world taking collective decision is an ideal position; but America and some other supporters of America wanted that there should be unilateralism. The idea that what America decides is best for the world is untrue, in multiple decision-making process including India, China, Asia Pacific and the Latin American countries, lies the future of peace in the world and by unilateralism, America decides with U.K., the future of mankind in the name of peace, justice and human rights that will create a worse situation in Asia including China-India relationship. As in these sensitive areas, multi-lateralism has no alternative. American unilateralism is a matter of temporary agenda. We have to oust these things by the collective efforts of humanity's conscience.

Yes, multi-lateralism has another fall out-- the political devolution. One may not believe that after 400 years of Westfellian world order, states came into existence. After the Second World War, one may not believe peace of political devolution that takes place in the empires and the former colonies. There are evidences of re-colonization and imperialisation might have been a possibility. Unknowingly, even India might have been brought under the orbit of the United States's vital interest not only in economic sense but also in political and other sense as well. So, mankind is facing the danger of re-colonization and re-imperialisation, and peace will be exiled if re-colonization happens.

We may come to economic globalization. Globalization is good. The capitalists, industrialists, economists thought out different meanings of globalization. Economic globalization in 1990 and 1991 has increased the gap between the poor and rich. America has also suffered from this. From the book on Globalization, I am stating these data. Only 1% rich American families have as much wealth as the other 95% bottom class Americans. It is untrue that all the Americans are rich, capitalists and industrialists. It is only 1%, the rest are all middle class though their quality of life may be much better than ours. Then, in this globalization advocacy, and perspective, more than 1.3 billion people survive with less than or equivalent to 1 dollar per day. 40 million go hunger every day. Half a million women die each year in childbirth. In Europe and Canada unemployment has risen to 11%.

Globalization has very noble intentions. But America-led globalization is taking a march on the soil of the planet. In Assam, in post-1991 economic liberalization that is also a step in globalization, employees in Assam and the northeastern states have not got their salaries. That the employees get their salaries after globalization is news. Every state government and every chief minister has the pre-conceived speech that the capital for development in the northeast is eaten up by the salaried persons. Globalization has given us results, but even then many of our economists and pro-American scholars are not ready to accept the ill effects of inequitable globalization. The globalization we have seen in the university, in the government service, on the roads, then in the productive sector is not good. Peasants are dying by committing suicide in Orissa due to globalization. In the present state of globalization, where unilateralism in the decision making process leads us towards unprecedented poverty, some middle class people don't have much suffering and pains in the hands of globalization.

Another thing the world is facing is, 'Clash of Civilisations' among Hindu, Buddhist, Christian civilisations and tribal civilisation. Samuel Huntington once a learned advisor to American government said that civilizations would clash and Islam is the common enemy of Europe, America and the rest of the world. And this theory has been taken over officially by the American Administration. The Iranian lady who has received Nobel Peace prize of 2003, recently in an interview given to BBC said that it is one or two persons of the faith who commit the fault, but do not point out fingers to any religion, Islam is not a fault. No religion is essentially a crime. We have to take lessons not from Samuel Huntington nor from Junior Bush. We cannot make and accept doctrines, which hits into the sovereignty of nations and states.

The globalization lesson is also a lesson for the northeast people. When we look into our political, cultural and economic status in progress, we have to see and hear people who can point out the merits and the demerits of globalisation. We should have the capacity-building and the capacity to form independent judgement on our own; and strangely, we have reached that stage. We can form independent judgement in the northeastern society on issues in the northeastern states.

The new world order has taught us a lesson. It has taught us the lesson that national questions have to be treated unlike you or someone treats terrorism and common criminals. Why evidence is required? In 1945, there were 50 countries. These 50 countries in 1945 had given birth to

140 children. 140 independent countries largely due to the de-colonization process in India, China, and the third world countries. We should see that the national questions have to be addressed though we have to consider the economic issue also. Colonization in any form has to be eradicated as we do with malaria. Similarly, we have to remove internal colonizations — be it external colonialism also.

The structure in the system is itself entrenched with violence. It does all the denial and deprivation, and all the movement--the legitimate movements are 'counter-violence to the violence', which is prevalent within the system, the constitution and within the civil society.

Whatever we see superficially is the violence in response to the counter-violence that is committed through denial, deprivation and inequitable distribution of wealth and political power through the so-called legitimate instruments of the constitution and many laws. Violence is hidden in the structure, in the civil society and in the instruments — that same matter and that same issue we have to study, when we study the Northeastern states.

For the sake of younger people, who don't know much about the history of the North-eastern states and not for the learned people, let me tell that in the book fair when I opened a Macmillan book and looked at a map which is meant for Class VII or VIII students, the map has very clearly marked that Assam and the other North-eastern states have been independent since the time before Christ till 1949 for some of parts, and for Assam till 1826. This is the curriculum of school geography, and we should restate the fact that Assam and the other northeastern states--seven states remained independent, centralised administration in the respective states and the countries;

so Assam had been a mainstream; Manipur, Tripura had been a mainstream. Similarly, Khasi and Jaintias were mainstreams.

Indian mainstream is not the only mainstream. Assam had its own mainstream with centralised administration for not less them 2000 years. But if we have to bring a mainstream into another bigger mainstream many things have to be worked out. That is why Gopinath Bordoloi wanted a separate constitution for Assam in 1946. He tried three times. I am sure Bordoloi was not a militant for his wanting a separate Constitution for Assam. Inherently, there are some systemic failures, there are some defects in the system, and the 'national question' has to be the central question of our discussion. We have to address to the 'Centrality of National Questions' in the restive N.E. region.

One should not vulgarise economy as the cause of militarisation or militancy. If poverty is the reason behind peripheral secessionalism in acquired territories, and if poverty is the cause of separatism in India, then Bihar for that matter which is one of the poorest states should be affected most. If one wants to separate Bihar from India then no one in Bihar will vote for this.

What is priority? Priority number one is the 'Centrality of National Question'. National questions in the northeastern states, are paramount and economic reasons, economic underdevelopment is complimentary. It is a collateral issue. But we cannot reserve the complimentary principle of economic reason and economic underdevelopment, and it cannot get primacy over the national question of Assam and the north-eastern states. These are vital things, which history has entrusted to us. It is not the speaker himself taking up an unfinished agenda in history. Assam had been a mainstream. Manipur, Tripura has been a mainstream. Now, if you want to bring these mainstreams into Indian mainstreams, there should be some adjustment of mainstreams, as there is not a not only one single mainstream.

Firstly, there is political pluralism, there is concept of f confederalism and India is a multinational country. If issues cannot be decided by leaders, by militant groups, by government, let the people decide. It is a democratic culture. Let the people of any state decide their own future. Why should you be afraid of the wishes of people? If people like to follow your agenda, people will vote for you. So, if the 'centrality of the national questions of the northeastern states could be resolved, economic questions could also be equally addressed, and in what ease, the first step to build up durable peace is the human rights standard in the north-east — the first step in a long journey in history.

Secondly, many people say that North-east's civil society has been militarised starting from the rebellion of the Manipur Communist Party in 1949 — the first insurgent movement in India and the region--the 100 gun Manipur Communist Party with the ideology of Maoism and with egalitarian economic slogan. After 7 to 8 years, in 1956-57 Naga Hills, Naga liberation war started. Then, it started in Tripura, Assam and Meghalaya.

The civil society in the Northeast has been totally militarised; and at the same time, as a response to militarisation, there were liberation wars, which are not terrorism. Of course, there are criminal gangs who have no hearts, who do not follow human rights and laws. We also agree that there are pockets of people who are violent and have no political cause, who have no messiahnic touch with human history and who have no commitment to history. But by and large, please accept the records of history that north-east's civil society has been militarised, and as a response to that militarisation with the presence of unprecedented imposition of all the imaginable black laws, the younger generation also responded with militarisation and not with terrorism.

We all agree that there are pockets of terrorists who are very unkind—very inhuman people, who commit crimes also; but 'liberation wars' and 'liberation groups are not terrorists. Alongside them, there are criminal gangs also, there are unlawful people, there are bad elements --we agree. But, the central issue is about militarisation and younger generations response to militarisation with 'liberation wars.' The question is about man's philosophy. Peripheral secessionism in acquired territories and separatism feeling is found prevalent in post-acquisition areas. Even if poverty is lurking in the lives of the Bihari or, that of a person of U.P., separatism-thinking does not exist there. There are historical reasons, historical experience and national contradictions, compounded by economic issues. We have to address the issue. If we are addressing to something collateral and non-significant, then we are not doing justice to the primary cause and the real issue.

How these are sorted out in other parts of the world? Yes, the other parts of the world can solve similar situations. Irist situation started in 1922. Now for more than 80 years the white people, the very rich Irist people fought against the British people. Poverty is not the cause, economy is not the cause, culture is not the cause, skin is not the cause but Irist people — learned people, highly educated people, highly volatile and highly civilized people fought against the British for a cause, for the historical cause, because Ireland was divided in 1922 by dividing Ireland into two and a part made, an independent entity. Poverty, unemployment may be one of the causes. If unemployment problem is the cause of separatism, then there are many unemployed youths in America. But it is not similar in the case of America.

The theory that I preach and you preach should be justifiable irrespective of the geography or the civilisation. The economic theory, the political theory, what is true here and what is untrue there is not a theory, but a hypothesis. Now, similarly, the Irist problem had been resolved in 1998 by adopting Good Friday Agreement. America was the guarantor. Similarly, the Palestinian problem will be sorted out soon, the process is there.

Then, for East Timor in Asia--through United Nations intervention the issue has been solved. If other countries and other nations can solve similar problems, why not India? This is a purely political issue. If the political issues are addressed, and the building blocks created, then peace and human rights will be there and the peace will be durable for centuries. This peace is not like that of Hitler. This peace can be seen in the horizon.

If the Timor problem could be solved, if the Ireland problem could be solved, if the Estonian problem could be solved in Soviet Union, why not in India under leadership. When Estonia with a few lakh population rose for separation if 1991, the Red Army and the KG B — the mightiest in the world — could have smashed it in one night. But they did not do, because it was a political issue. This will not happen simply with statesmanship, but with the reasoning and will power of the statesmanship.

The problem is largely created by the misgovernance

by New Delhi. They should resolve the problem and remove the debris from the history, and they should try to solve the 'national contradiction' as quickly, and as firmly as possible, so that durable and just peace and human rights can be restored in the region.

3

Human Rights in Armed Conflict Areas: Standard Setting and Binding Obligations

Human rights policy of India depends on the perception of the government and the civil society as to what the constitution and the laws have sofar provided for on the one hand, on the level of compliancc with the binding human rights conventions on the other hand and the national commitment. The state obligations and individual criminal responsibility co-exist in the human rights and humanitarian laws regime. The NE region faces a situation of armed conflict for half a century, undergoes militarization of civil society and political repercussions of significance, which calls for resolution. The repressive laws have been found to be counter-productive to the peculiar political issue that sustains like a festering wound. Besides, the government of India has binding obligations to human rights conventions and political responsibility in fulfilling national commitments. Human rights policy has to be holistic and be compatible with the objective realities.

PERIPHERAL SECESSIONISM

The objective reality in the North-Eastern region of India is quite obvious for the last half a century. *Firstly,* the large chunk of the North-Eastern region has been acquired in post-British period or, had been otherwise excluded areas, not governed by the metropolitan administration. *Secondly,* subsequently thereafter, militant peripheral secessionism had started the kick off in no time. *Thirdly,* brutal state repression or state terrorism had been let loose in the regional civil society for neutralizing the insurgents, thereby militarizing the entire civil society.

By the repressive measures the administration and the security forces had adopted, the civil society has been alienated from the administration; anti-colonial agenda has been advanced consequent upon the state repression. The civil society has to carry a heavy baggage of black laws, undreamt of for half a century. The human rights policy that could be set by the union government has to take into account boldly and unfailingly, the hard objective realities and the historical specifics of the region.

How the union government could perceive of the deep-rooted political question or national questions of the NE region, and address successfully to the core issues that sparked off the insurgency or belligerency whatsoever could not be delinked absolutely from the objective realities on the one hand and the firmly established, universally accepted human rights benchmarks, endorsed by the constitutional norms. In one word, the government may not be doing its best in violating the universally accepted or even binding human rights laws--national or, international, in the pretext of integrating the acquired territories to the mainstream.

A fair, just and durable political solution could lead to resolving the festering peripheral secessionism and while doing so, accepted human rights standards have to be honoured to the fullest extent Draconian laws like the infamous AFSPA — Armed Forces Special Powers Act, 1958, among others, have to be repealed forthwith in the same way as the not so infamous POTA has been scrapped. The National Human Rights Commission of India had long back recommended the repeal of the AFSPA and the enlightened world public opinion stands for the repel. Justice delayed is justice denied to 40 million people of the NE region. Human rights policy should have to reflect the urgency of the need for the repeal of the infamous law.

In the long history of state repression, extrajudicial executions, arbitrary detentions, torture, third degree methods, and the collective mental traumatization, the civil society reacted vehemently against the black laws and the forces - the armed wing of the government. Sharmila is fasting for nearly five years and Chittaranjan has self-immolated last year in protest against the AFSPA; the new generation is waiting in the queue to protest against the terror let loose by the government.

In Assam, reportedly 265 Assamese citizens had been executed under a secret killing agenda, which newspapers attribute to the secret decree of either the Home Ministry of India or state agencies and the matter lies before the Supreme Court. Many more events of similar kind happened in Nagaland and elsewhere in the NE region. The question of accountability of the government and institutional immunity of the security forces or other invisible forces whatsoever have not been addressed to appropriately and in time. Is the NE region the iron curtain or Auschwitz of India is a million dollar question for sensible people. What has happened to national and international obligations to the standard setting and protection of human rights is another query that awaits for full reply from the person in the seats of power.

EMBEDDED POLITICAL IMMORALITY

Human rights policy as a desired goal of people-friendly, participatory good governance is circumscribed by the binding national and international obligations of the government of India. It has to put to task, the embedded political immorality, which any over- patriotic government would succumb to on the misconceived grounds of expediency One cannot simply commit genocide or, conceal human torture chambers in the name of patriotism as President Milosevic or, Idi Amin or, the great Führer did to their undesirable population groups. The human rights policy of India ought to be made honourable, fair, just and durable, while making it fully compatible with the universal standard and defined benchmarks. The state responsibility, obligations, among others, are concretized:

Firstly, the binding constitutional obligations

Sanctity of life and property of citizens and persons has been guaranteed by the Constitution of India; even the permissible derogation in public emergency situations is governed by reasonable, fair and just procedure established by law. The apex court in its 1997 verdict in upholding the AFSPA has overlooked the qualifying parameters of reasonableness in constructing *the procedure established by law*. It has approved the killing by soldier, of any citizen in the NE region on mere suspicion as justified, and implicitly approved suspicion as the best legal basis for deprivation of human life, contrary to well established common law rules.

A line of thought has evolved out of the bad judgement. A capitalist judge shall always reject a communist law and *vice versa*. A widely circulated policy input is: had the five-member apex court in 1997 comprised only the ethnic cousins of Manorama or Sharmila or Chittranjan, the bench should have rejected 'suspicion' as the valid legal basis of shooting down to death a North-Easterner, while interpreting the procedure established under law in article 21 of the Constitution, and rejected the AFSPA outright as the relic of Zurrasic-park justice.

The deep-rooted issue is about the man, who runs the justicing apparatus. In Dred Scot case, the US Supreme Court has accepted the Afrikan-American as a commodity in the 19th century. The judicial policy has apparently justified state terrorism in the pretext of his brand of nationalism. Future generation would have be amazed at the apex court's wonderful endorsement of suspicion as a valid legal basis for state's deprivation of life.

Secondly, the binding human rights treaties

Human rights treaties including the ICCPR, 1966 and, the ICESCR, 1966, among others, which the government of India had signed and ratified are binding to India in the capacity of a respectable member of the international community. Several of the vital provisions of the binding conventions have been overlooked consistently. Article 4 of the ICCPR forbids the government of India including its constitutional creature—the apex court and the judiciary, to deprive of life of persons and citizens even in the most formidable situation of *public emergency*.

Public emergency has not been officially proclaimed as required by the binding conventions in the NE region for half a century; accountability of all the state agencies to the parliament for all the acts and omissions in the region conducted during the officially proclaimed public emergency has been abdicated unlawfully, and the United Nations has not been notified for the governmental actions. The apex court in 1997 has fully abdicated giving necessary attention to this public emergency requirement under the law. The reasons for the apex court's overlooking the vital aspect of law are not known.

Thirdly, the mandate of humanitarian regime

The four Geneva Conventions, 1949 are binding to a signatory like the government of India and the Geneva Convention Act, 1960 has been enacted accordingly. The Indian statute calls for amendment in order to make it functional.

The common article 3 of the four conventions forbids the state agencies and the state like India to deprive of life of non-participants in the non-international armed conflicts and citizens without judicial guarantees, to torture and to kidnap, among others. The apex court has missed in 1997, its rare opportunity to vindicate the judicial guarantee, it has to afford to citizens of the NE region against the state repression and brutality. The state should not abdicate its state responsibility under all circumstances.

The non- state actors (NSA) or, entities whosoever barring the mindless terrorists, operating in the armed conflict zone in the region have also certain ethical humanitarian responsibility to comply with the common article 3. Should they not conform to the benchmarks of engagements, and penalize the non-combatants or members of the civil society, they would earn the label of terrorism. The NSAs—n'one-state actors' should not evade humanitarian responsibility under one false pretext or other. Once India becomes a party to the ICC treaty, the immunity the NSAs enjoy today has to go. Human rights policy is yet to articulate the aspect.

Fourthly, individual criminal responsibility

The international community has ushered in an era of terminating immunity and impunity of individuals — be he a soldier or army chief or a prime minister or a guerrilla leader of the NSA-committing *heinous* international crimes. The Rome ICC treaty, 1998 is functioning to do the job leaving aside powerful countries like the USA and India outside its fold as pariah, because of their ambiguous and ambivalent stance towards retaining immunity and impunity of their heinous national and international criminals. The benchmark of this century's international rule of law and international criminal justice lies in the ICC, which the government of India considers as untouchable or a liability. In one word, the government's stand encourages commission of heinous international crimes as the world's only supercop power does around the world with millions of human skeletons in uncle Sam's cupboard for democracy. India, particularly — Gandhian India ought to act differently in this imnumity-termination job of the U.S.A.

Fifthly, re-activation of the national institutions

The national responses to the universal human rights standard is desperately poor and as a result, the national human rights institutions including the national state commissions have not delivered the goods as desired by the civil society. The statutes, the functions, the manpower and the objectives enunciated for the machineries call for radical reforms. Even the defence forces can not be brought to the jurisdiction of the NHRC of India thereby legitimizing immunity and impunity at the institutional level. Too little done, vast undone.

POLICY DIMENSIONS

By taking a thread from the principle of fair and good governance based on fair and proportional representation in multi-racial and multi-national India, the objective social reality as found is that a mere 1 to 2 % of the Indian defence forces is drawn from amongst the Muslims which constitute 20% of the population and also that the Northern-Southern racial axis in the last half a century denied a Naga to be the President and a Manipuri to be Prime minister of India, we take a leaf out from the racialist brand of power-sharing in the republic.

There is no suitable explanation except the justification of racism in disguise. It would be better to stop this discrimination. The subject people rise against the new Moghuls. The false justification for denial and deprivation is as good as lawyer's paradise. The regime is simply covertly pro-Nazi, which is perecived as a perpetual terror to the national minorities. The rest is political gimmick.

The universally established right to development and the right of the legitimate people to self-determination, among others, have not been justifiably and properly addressed to, thereby facilitating a mere prairie fire in Naga hills, sparked off by the AFSPA, 1958, to spread the insurgency wildfire across the NE region. The message is as simple as the panic of AFSPA dragon running berserk in the NE civil society. The damage done to the texture and fabric has nearly become irreversible in spite of periodic economic packages announced for the region and distribution of a bundle of *tamvapatra* to willing subject of hidden racism.

Dissemination

The national institutions, human rights machineries and the multi-media, and the NGOs can play important roles in dissemination of anti-racism, anti-casteism, anti-minorityism to the power elites, policy makers, opinion makers and grassroot social workers. The Nazi brand of institutional hatred of minorities and tribes has to be wiped out from the majoritarian mind-set and politics. The mind-set of the power elite has been infected deeply by the psychic HIV and AIDS for the last several centuries. The issues about the right to development and right of the people of the NE region to self- determination have not been properly and in time, addressed to by the powers that be.

The institutional aberrations from the human rights standard, followed and adopted universally call for corrections. The apex court, the legislature, the executive and the defence forces have to correct the intentional or unintentional deviations from the universal human rights standard. Accountability has to be fixed and penal actions or otherwise may be found necessary for booking the wilful human rights violaters. However, the culture of impunity has not been terminated.

The governments and the national institutions have to fully and adequately comply with the binding human rights treaties to which India has been a party. The governmental neglect is obvious in several compulsory-reporting obligations. A glaring example is cited. The government of India has failed deliberately to furnish the Fourth India Report due by 2000 even today, to the UN Human Rights Committee. Nobody in the country whosoever including the activist NGOs could find time to raise the blatant failure and take up actions.

On the recommendation of the National Human Rights Commission of India, the government of India had the opportunity to repeal the AFSPA, 1958 long before the benign POTA has been repealed. The necessity of the Prime Minister to constitute a panel to review the black law in 2005 following the June 18 volcanic eruption in Manipur has been redundant after considering the primacy of the National Human Rights Commission over an ad hoc panel.

Every one knows that the 1958 black law is Lord Linlithgow's dirty colonial law to smash the Indians in NE region down to the roots. The promulgation of repressive colonial law leads to no other conclusion than that colonialism exists in the NE region. If colonialism exists, liberation movements logically follow. Is there any other alternative conclusion is difficult to rediscover.

Unlike other rogue states of the world, which rise above universal laws and principles, India has been and continues to be a role model and an inspiration of the one time Non-aligned movement, and leader of the newly emerging developing countries. There is a difference between the USA signing or not signing the ICC Rome treaty, 1998, and Gandhian India provoking the international community as American clone in being apathetic to the Rome treaty, 1998 by inventing unacceptable false arguments of one kind or another.

The union government could be urged upon to sign and ratify the ICC Rome treaty, 1998. It has to repeal the AFSPA, 1958, which is basically a colonial, repressive law aimed at perpetuating colonialism in the country. The government of India also bears profound moral responsibility to sign and ratify basic humanitarian laws like the Additional Protocols to the Geneva Conventions, 1977.

Time has come to re-educate the bureaucracy, the ministry, the media and the defence personnel with the universal human rights standards and ramifications of human rights violations. The state human rights commissions have to be re-charged and re-activated.

The government of India has the primary responsibility to comply with its earlier national commitments and human rights obligations. It has to fully endorse the universally accepted human rights treaties by signing and ratifying the other significant conventions. The human rights policy should be holistic and multilateral, urge upon accountability, transparency and followup actions of the national institutions and officials.

4

Revisiting Justice Reddy Report on Armed Forces Special Powers Act, 1958

After prolonged, sustained mass agitation in Manipur in 2004 demanding the repeal of the controversial statute, the prime minister constituted Justice Jeevan Reddy committee, which in its report submitted in 2005 had recommended the repeal of the Armed Forces [Special Powers] Act, 1958. The statute is critically re-visited in the comprehensive sense of the term, in the brief article.

State parties including India is under International and national obligations under Article 2 of the International Covenant on Civil and Political Rights (ICCPR) to enforce the ICCPR.[1] By invoking the AFSPA, 1958 for half a century in the NE region, the union government has consistently not complied with the binding public emergency provisions of Article 4 of the ICCPR, which the Supreme Court, in its 1997 verdict, has comfortably overlooked.

I. OVERVIEW OF REDDY REPORT, 2005

The prime minister of India had constituted in November 2004, a five-member committee under the chairmanship of former justice of Supreme Court Sri B.P. Jeevan Reddy[2] to examine the AFSPA, in the wake of prolonged mass movements led by *Apunba Lup* [United Organization in Manipur] demanding immediate repeal of the aforesaid statute. The terms of reference of the committee are:

> Keeping in view the legitimate concerns of the people of the North-Eastern region, the need to foster Human Rights keeping in perspective the imperatives of security and maintenance of public order to review the provisions of the Armed Forces [Special Powers] Act, 1958 as amended in 1972 and to advise the Govt. of India Whether-

(a) To amend the provisions of the Act to bring them in consonance with the obligations of the Govt. towards protection of Human Rights; or

(b) To replace the Act by a more humane Act.[3]

The Armed Forces [Special Powers) Act, 1958 [AFSPA hereafter] has triggered off nationwide debate for substantially long period and drew international attention largely from the international human rights NGOs, and the United Nations Human Rights Committee, among others. Following the molestation, gangrape and extrajudicial murder of Kumari Th. Manorama[4] in Manipur, by the Assam Rifles personnels on 11 July, 2001, and the fast unto death undertaken by Kumari Irom Sharmila[5] in Manipur since September, 2001 in protest against spraying of bullets by the armed forces to death to several bystanders at a public bus stop at Malom in the outskirt of Imphal city in 2001, and mass civil agitations launched thereafter for the repeal of the AFSPA, the Central government set-up a five-member committee under the chairmanship of former Supreme Court judge — Mr Justice B.P. Jeevan Reddy on 19 November, 2004. [The recommendation of the

Report is appended].

The extra-judicial executions of innocent civilian populace and commission of other forms of naked human rights violations remain a fact of life in the North-Eastern states in India for the last five decades. Two contentious stances are being advanced by the state, which has rationalized the enactment and enforcement of demonical law like the AFSPA 1958 (Armed Forces Special Powers Act, 1958 — AFSPA, hereafter), and by the defenders of human rights, who not only defy the apparent legitimacy of such a law, but also raise the politico-historical basis of the upsurges, that characterize the North-Eastern civil society.

The apex court upheld the statute on 27 November, 1997, by overlooking the gross human rights violations since 1958, whereas it could have struck down the black law on the grounds of its manifest incompatibility with the Rule of Law and the ICCPR, 1966 to which India is a state party. Justice Jeevan Reddy report 2005(report hereafter) observes:

> "{the} Act, for whatever reason, has become a symbol of oppression, an object of hate and an instrument of discrimination and highhandedness."[6] It further observes — "The Court does not—it is not supposed to pronounce upon the wisdom or the necessary of such an enactment."[7]
>
> Although the armed forces do not favour repeal of the black law — the AFSPA, the report has recorded the assessment of the armed forces about the political consequences of the AFSPA;
>
> "Army:...(a) The insurgency situation in the north-east has worsened since the AFSPA has been applied in the 1950s. The insurgent groups have greatly increased. Their cadres, weapons, tactical capabilities have expanded and improved immediately."[8]

> Apparently, the black law has acted as surrogate mother of increasingly proliferating belligerency and insurgency.
>
> The deployment of forces has been re-examined by the government of India.
>
> "Ministry of Home Affairs: In its presentation to the Committee, the MHA stated that Armed Forces and other forces of the centre would be progressively withdrawn from the north-east,. . ."[9] An impartial analysis of these official statements of the respectable national institutions of India reveals that they incidentally remain rhetorical at their best.

Indian state, unlike the Indian nationhood is a nascent British-created entity, which has passed through diverse—and even, non-complimentary historical experiences. A nation-in-the-making that India is, Manipur state and Tripura state have been brought to the fold of the nascent state after two years of Indian independence; the other states of the region remained parts of Assam, which on its part, joined the British Indian mainstream in 1826. Mainstream historians had possibly misrepresented the acquired territories of the NE region as state succession from the British colonial power.

In political terms, the sub-terranean faultlines are apparently cracking up, and Indian state persists in quick-fixing the deep-structured NSGT [Non-Self-Governing — Territories in international law] faultlines with the help of the powerful Indian army and state repression, which would loose legitimacy without invoking demoniacal laws like the AFSPA, and the Punjab Security Act 1953, among a host of others. Occasional patchwork and cosmetic reforms apart, the deep-structured political contradictions are shelved beyond the reach of perceptive and visionary stroke of statesmanship, which itself is a missing word in the colonial legacy.

The report takes a look into the legacy of draconian laws adopted in India:

> "To meet the situation arising in certain parts of India on account of the partition of the country in 1947, the Government of India issued four ordinances viz., the Bengal Disturbed Areas (Special Powers of Armed Forces) Ordinance, 1947; the Assam Disturbed Areas (Special Powers of Armed Forces Ordinance), 1947 (Act of 1947); the East Punjab and Delhi Disturbed Areas (Special Powers of Armed Forces) Ordinance, 1947 (Act 17 of 1947); and the United Provinces Disturbed Areas(Spacial Powers of Armed Forces) Ordinance, 1947 (Act 22 of 1947). These Ordinances were replaced by the Armed Forces (Special Powers) Act 1948 being Act 3 of 1948.)[10]

The tangible political repercussions of the invocation of the AFSPA demonstrate the following phenomena: *Firstly,* the correlation of the demoniacal law with its political corollary is found in subsequent political fallouts. The AFSPA's predecessor — the Armed Forces Special Powers Ordinance, 1942 had been enacted in order to neutralize quit-India movement. It was hundred percent a colonial instrument, ušed for legitimization and continuation of Salt water colonialism. The British colonial Armed Forces [Special Powers) Ordinance, 1942 promulgated by Viceroy Linlithgow[: sic. self-style as Lord] had provided: " 2(l) Any officer not below the rank of captain in His Majesty's Military Force..., require any personnel under his command to use force as may be necessary, even to the causing of death, against any person...".

The Indian parliament had acted virtually as Linlithgow -II in the North-Eastern region for half a century. The 1942 demoniacal ordinance crafted by the British colonialists, among others, had expedited and facilitated the passage of Indian Independence Act, 1947. The 1958 law inherits the same powerful political potency.

Secondly, the AFSPA, 1958 has been enacted in 1958 in order to quell the ethnic uprising in the tiny Naga Hills district in the then unfractured Assam. After four decades, like a nuclear chain-reaction, the invocation of the black law in a small range of hills spread over the conflagration like domino effect in all the seven states. It has the potency of flaring-up politically sensitive issues like prairie-fire. The civil society in the region had perceived for whatever reason it can perceive of, the custodians of law — the armed forces as a symbol of terror which virtually invited the new generation to fight back for šelf-protection and self-preservation; and the black law had become the breeding ground of a large number of rebel outfits, which later on have evolved their own course of action and reasons. By now, it has become irreversible.

II. TWO-HOUR SUMMARY PARLIAMENTARY DEBATE

Concentration Camp Theory

In spite of referring the bill to a JOINT PARLIAMENTARY COMMITTEE to examine the merits and possible political consequences of invoking the statute and discussing the same in details, on the fateful 18th August, 1958, the AFSPA had been adopted in great haste after a meagre two hour-long summary debate by the parliament.[11] Manipur MP Sri L. Achaw Singh argued against the bill, "This is a black law....How can we imagine that these military officers should be allowed to shoot to kill and without warrant arrest and search? This is a lawless law."[12]

Manipur hill MP Rungsung Suisa argued against the AFSPA, "All these Ordinances and sending of Armed Forces will not solve the problem".[13]

MP Sri Warior (Trichur) opposed the bill, — "The whole of Assam and Manipur is going to come under Martial Law though the Martial Law and an emergency are not declared."[14]. In the same vein, MP Sri Mahanty opposed the bill, —"What I am trying to submit is that this is a martial law'. He further argued, "... But, we do not want a free India with barbed wires and concentration camps, where the Havildars can shoot at sight any man".[15] However, brute majoritarianism of the ruling Congress got the bill passed without conducting a soul-searching, elaborate debate.

III. EMERGENCY UNPROCLAIMED

MPs opposed the the invocation of unproclaimed emergency through the backdoor. MP Mahanty opposed the bill,—"It has to be conceded that there are enough materials to show that there is an emergency. But the Emergency provisions of the Constitution have been invoked without the President declaring an Emergency."[16].

In similar vein, MP Dr. Krishnaswami opposed the bill,—"This is a state of affairs that can be brought about only by a Proclamation of Emergency promulgated under article 352 of the Constitution. The Bill seeks to circumvent these provisions and attempts to usurp the powers of the state not warranted by the Constitution."[17] He further argued,—"I suggest, here, the unconstitutionality is so patent that we are justified in requesting the Chair to rule that the measure is ultra vires."[18]

The state and security forces have also been conditioned to demoniacal-law-dependency so much so that the state feels deeply vulnerable without resorting to unproclaimed emergency and spacial power laws. It is comparable euphemistically to the addicts' drug dependency. The decision-makers in the state and security forces have evolved a different sort of hyper-subjective perception in regard to the unresolved political question of historical importance. The distorted perceptions are indicated by the following official projections:

I. The security forces are fighting low-intensity war against ANEs (Anti National Elements, as they are known to the army — the insurgents (ANE for enemy);

II. In aid of the civil authority, the forces assume the power for internal security management on par with defence against external aggression;

III. The forces use military power so as to quick-fix the fault lineš, inherited from colonial history;

IV. The armed forces need additional empowerment like the AFSPA, and other concomitant draconian laws in order to maintain public order the extra-judicial power for execution of any suspected citizen under section 4 of the AFSPA and virtual immunity of the extrajudicial killers from prosecution under section 6 of the same statute;

V. In doing so, the forces should not be dragged into allegations of human rights-violations before the justicing system under the normal rule of law, while the forces have their own court-martial system;

VI. The forces, deployed by the third largest army in the world against a few hundreds of politically motivated secessionists can not be considered to have been deployed in excess of the requirement of military necessity;

VII. Human rights violations are not atrocities, but a modest inconvenience, to be bore by the patriotic

> civilian population: These routine violations are considered a military necessity so as to keep the country in tact. Euphemistically speaking, patriotism has been constructed so as to include uncomfortable things like extrajudicial executions and torture of suspects whosoever.

The reasons had espoused the same set of strong arguments in a post-colonial country, advanced at the time of enactment and invocation of the colonial Armed Forces Special Powers Ordinance in 1942 by the imperial power, who desired the British to keep the empire in tact. The obvious contradiction lies in the fact that the justification for colonization or, re-colonization through colonial statute after the lapse of the colonialism has been a badly argued case. The demoniacal colonial law had to exist in order to sustain NSGT or, colony and conversely, the invocation of colonial statute proves that the colony survives in some parts of the country even after the British left India in 1947. Colonial repression cannot exist unless there are colonies; the burden of proof lies with the law-makers of colonial repressive laws in post-colonial state.

The central issue, which resulted to insurgency or, national liberation movement — as it has been known to the insurgents or, in the parlance of universal de-colonization process — in the mindset of the law makers-probably leads to the enactment of the draconian law, and shaped the attitude of the army, who had been given additional empowerment for extra-judicial execution of the citizens as well the suspects under the AFSPA.

The deep-rooted political issue has been misconceived as 'law and order' or, at most 'internal security' issue, whereas it bears the intrinsic essence of de-colonization and national liberation war. The issue remains very deep and the fault-lineš characterized by national questions are profound. The sustenance of the issue for fives decades itself indicates that human rights violations and the twisted perceptions are merely symptoms of the chronic malaise. The Annual Report of Home Ministry, Government of India 1996-97 and subsequent other observations report about the states most affected by insurgent activities of various militant groups. The union government, has therefore, arranged for talks with a Nagaland liberation movement-outfit since 1997, and the political process continues.

The available evidence, the demand-structure, the historical facts and the pattern of union governments response to the political issue make it amply clear that the decades-old political violence, as espoused by the insurgents or liberation army of the NSGT, has been a consequence or manifestation of unresolved or, insufficiently addressed political question from the time of Indian Independence in 1947.

Historical evidence[19] sufficiently corroborated by texts, documents and instruments clearly stipulates that -

(I) Manipur and Tripura had been annexed to the Indian political fold, in 1949 after two years of Indian independence;

(II) Assam became a part of British India — not by her choice — but by the choice of Burma and British, which signed the Treaty of Yandaboo in 1826[20], without the consent or any form of concurrence whatever of independent Assam [Asom since 2006];

(III) the ethnic tribes which remained in the excluded hill areas of Assam fused themselves in the last five decades into nationhood, and claimed independence prior to the passage of Indian Independence Act 1947[21], and

(IV) British-created republic of India, which has graduated from dominion status to union status has been a totally different entity from the original Indian [Hindusthani] nation that continued for centuries in the Gangetic basin — the *Aryabrata*.

The British-created India has been a deliberate political creation, unlike the virtually homogenous Indian nation, based on Aryabrata. The issue is, therefore, rooted in historical facts, arguments, legacy and imperatives compatible with that of the NSGT elsewhere in the world.

(V) The accords, reached and breached between national groups and the government during the last five decades, being purely political issues in all sense of the term, remain beyond the reach of the wide arms of the apex court or, human rights commissions or, the instruments of the civil government. Since 1997, the union government has initiated political moves by holding dialogue with one of the liberation outfits of Nagaland. Even after 9 years of talks, no substantive result or positive indication whatsoever has so far emerged. However, the union government relentlessly bring more rebel groups into its fold by trapping them into the similar stagnant situations thereby yielding no result of substance.

The report inches into the root of the political turbulence in the NE region. It observes:

> "4]. The committee feels that the agitations such as those in Manipur and elsewhere are merely symptoms of a malaise which goes much deeper. The recurring phenomena of one agitation after another over various issues and the

fact that public sentiments can be roused so easily and frequently to unleash unrest, confrontation and violence, also points to deep rooted causes which are often not addressed. Unless the core issues are tackled, any issue or non-issue may continue to trigger another upsurge or agitation."[22]

The human right violations following the invocation of special demoniacal laws and state repression for nearly half-a-century has been inextricably associated with the relevant political question. The issue, therefore, stands for the closest political scrutiny; however, the enactment of special laws, invocation of half-a-century old emergency laws without formal declaration of emergency have to be assessed on the basis of 'rule of law' entrenched in Indian constitutionalism and accepted standards of civilized jurisprudence.

Armed Conflicts for Half a Century

After the government of India deployed Indian armed forces in the 1950s to quell the insurgency in the Naga hills, and subsequently thereafter to all the places in the entire NE region, recurrent armed conflicts occurred in the region for half a century between the state armed forces and the armed forces of the National Liberation Movements. The deployment of the armed forces are reported in the parliament, multi-media, cabinet papers and by all the for a throughout the world. On occasions, the Army Corps commanders released PIB reports stating the status of the ongoing armed conflicts along with the army's success stories over the armed guerrillas.

The invocation of the AFSPA since 1958 and even prior to that period, the Unlawful Activities (Prevention) Act, 1967, the National Security Act and a dozen of draconian laws for a long period, the annual reports placed in the parliament by the Home Ministry about the death of Indian soldiers and the guerrillas or extremists with facts and figures, unambiguously prove the existence of armed conflicts between the state forces and the liberation guerrillas. The government-controlled media routinely broadcast the reports of engagements between the state forces and the guerrillas.

Besides, India's periodic reports submitted to the UN treaty bodies for several decades clearly stipulate the armed conflicts events and the treaty bodies have recorded the occurrences. The apex court in its 1997 verdict had also admitted that insurgency and armed struggles occurred in the NE region. In innumerable international seminars and conferences, the government of India had placed the occurrences in the government's own suitable version. Human rights organizations in the country and abroad had routinely censured the crimes committed by the Indian state forces in the region for half a century.

Notwithstanding the hard facts and realities, in the deliberation about the implementation of UN Security Council resolution no. 1325, the government of India representative, in his report placed before the CEDAW in 2007, reversed the aforementioned facts and denied the existence of armed conflicts in the NE region, particularly in the state of Manipur. The representative has reversed all the commitments given by the attorney general of India in the 1991 and 1997 to the UN Human Rights Commit, and gave a clean chit to the blatant violation of human rights of women committed by the forces for half a century.

Humanitarian Laws

The report records the evidence of grave violation of humanitarian laws in these words: "There have been a large number of cases where those taken away without warrants have "disappeared", or ended up dead or badly injured. Suspicion and bitterness have grown as a result."[23]

The remedies suggested by the committee are found to be deficient. It has not gone far into the domain of humanitarian laws in armed conflict situations; however, it has suggested:

> "[7. As stated hereinabove], the ULP (*sic.* Unlawful Activities Prevention) Act, does contemplate, by necessary implication, use of armed forces or para-military forces to conduct operations and to take steps to fight and curb terrorism. It does not, however, contain any provision specifying their powers, duties and procedures relevant to their deployment. It does not also provide for an internal mechanism *ensuring accountability of such forces* with a view to guard against *abuses and excesses by delinquent members of such forces.* It is this lacuna, which is to be supplied by inserting appropriate provisions in the ULP Act. The provision so introduced should be clear, unambiguous and must specify the powers of the armed forces /para military forces while acting to curb terrorist/ insurgent activities."[24] [emphasis added]

The sustained use of armed forces for half a century and even more naturally and unambiguously in the NE region implies the need for invoking international humanitarian laws, as the standard state practice suggests in the standard setting process. The lack of accountability or immunity and excesses committed by the state forces have been cited by the report; the union government has not fully addressed to these preponderant issues. The basic legal materials are therefore, discussed below.

The imperative need for the government to abide by the International bill of human rights arises out of constitutional requirement, general customary International law, common law background, state practices and above all, the union government's signature and ratification of the two covenants, 1966 on 10 April, 1979.

The bindingness of human-rights law on the part of the union government and its Instruments like the security forces or the judiciary etc. arises out of the following norms, national obligations and ensured compliance:

I. Provisions of articles 253, 51,246, schedule VII list I items 10-15, among others, of the Constitution of India;

II. State practices starting from India's becoming a member of the United Nations in 1945, even before two years of her independence;

III. General and customary International law, Jus Cogens as followed by the comity and community of nations, of which India is an inseparable part;

IV. The supreme court of India's endorsement of the human rights covenants of the United Nations in the process of evolving 'human rights jurisprudence' in several landmark public interest litigation cases; and the apex courts endorsement of the human rights covenants by incorporation as part of particular fundamental right, is found in the apex court statement in PUCL vs. Union of India (1977)2 JT 3/1/l), among others;

V. Fundamental rights under chapter III of the Constitution which can no longer be suspended even during a situation of emergency, following the 44th amendment of the Constitution;

VI. Article 21, compounded with articles 14 and 19 of the Constitution that has been placed as a special class of mini-code, especially after the construction of 'due process of law' thereby meaning the 'procedure duly established by law' Procedure established by law ought to be just, fair, reasonable and not arbitrary. Several apex court verdicts have qualified the procedure established by law.

VII. Rule of law, democracy and judicial review remain the basic features of the Constitution, unlike peripheral and unsustainable special laws, which do not conform to the basic tenets of rule of law.

Human rights covenants, signed and ratified by the union government of India are no longer convenient appendages or one time disposable bags, which could be dispensed with, whenever found inconvenient. They are increasingly indispensable. Civilized international comity expects India to act differently from the USA and other ROQUE states of the world. India has been NAM leader for 130 countries and accepted harbinger for world peace, non-violence and International morality unlike the USA. The union government of India conveniently chooses to abandon herself and her super eminent values for the sake of winning petty political and localized wars over the helpless people of the NE region.

The international standard of human rights, which has been crystallised by the Constitution and International bill of human rights, has to be complied with by the union government and its civil as well as military instrumentalities. In the case of the compliance or non-compliance whatsoever, the union government has been placed for reporting obligations under article 40 of the ICCPR, 1966. The union government has so far submitted three periodic reports to the UN Human Rights Committee and the Fourth report which was due by 2001, as reported by the committee has not been submitted till 2006. The delay reflects India's utter neglect of ICCPR obligations under Article 2 and 40.

Besides constitutional and legal accountability, the union government is politically accountable to the comity of nations for the maintenance of 'peace' and 'security', as envisaged by the UN Charter, the violation of which could be made a subject matter of the UN instrumentalities including the action of the UN Security Council. Just because India is having one of the largest army in the world and special laws empowering the army to commit covert or, overt genocide, it can not waive its accountability towards the maintenance of peace and security in the world with impunity, by resorting to state repression of the dependent populace — of the NSGT (NON -Self-Governing Territories), overlooked by the UN, which is seemingly apathetic to NSGT of South Asia.

The union government of India had recognized a number of national liberation outfits or, insurgent groups as bodies demanding secession from the country vide the Unlawful Activities (Prevention) Act 1967 and other similar laws. The statute has paradoxically given recognition to the national liberation outfits as bodies fighting a war of independence and secession from the union of India.

Periodically, notice has been publicly issued by the state to these NLM/NSL bodies through dailies in order to lend testimony to the fact that they demand separation from India and claim their national independence. The series of governmental gazettes, notices and publications, by implication, label that these outfits are merely 'gonds', 'criminals'— provocateurs of 'law and order' problem and both the parties, interlocked in insurgency and counter-insurgency armed-conflicts endorse the same view point that outfits demand independence from India and they resort to 'Any means available with them' in the process of their national liberation struggle. International humanitarian laws become, therefore, relevant in the context of the governmental recognition of the outfits as political organizations, committed to a political cause and undertaking armed conflicts in pursuit of their national independence.

The prevailing International Humanitarian Laws invariably stipulate the following universal standards, which even in the event of their violations or grave breach, do not lose their standing legitimacy:

I. The four Geneva Conventions, 1949, signed by the union government of India and Indian enactment of Geneva Convention Act 1960 render that the International Humanitarian Laws are applicable to India and its armed forces;

II. The protection of life, liberty and property of the civilians, *hors de combat* is non-derogable under common article 3 of the Conventions to which the government of India is a party, and the two Protocols. World Court (ICJ) has endorsed these rights as *jus cogens*, and the same under customary international law (Nicaragua vs. USA, 1986);

III. The government of India has been disempowered under Common article 3 of the four Geneva Conventions, 1949 to commit extra-judicial execution of persons without judicial guarantees. The Supreme Court missed the opportunity to see that AFSPA be struck down, as it is incompatible with common article 3 of Geneva Conventions and ICCPR article 4. The judiciary has failed its duty in this context by overlooking 'judicial guarantees' as required by Common article 3 of the four Geneva Conventions. (see also Martens clause). The Common article 3 of the 4 Geneva Conventions binding to the government of India and by extended constitutional construction, to the Supreme Court of India, provides the law as follows:

> Common article 3(1).... "To this end, the following acts are and shall remain prohibited at any time and in any place [*sic.* NE included] whatsoever with respect to the above-mentioned persons [*sic.* persons taking no part in hostilities]:
>
> (a) violence to life and person,.."
>
> (d) " the passing of sentences and the carrying out of executions without previous judgement pronounced by a regularly constituted court,...".

IV. The Supreme Court judgment in NPMHR vs. Union of India, 27 November, 1997 has laid down guidelines in para 56-58; these guidelines cannot be violated, but has also been violated recurrently. Children under 18 years have also been extra-judicially executed for half a century in violation of laws and Conventions and in blatant violations of right of the child convention.

V The insurgents and national liberation movements (NLMs) had been admittedly accepted as subjects of International law, especially after the decolonization movements since the 1960s. It might be recalled that both the former USSR and the state of India hammered out the first GA 'Right of the people to Self-determination' resolution in 1960 Since the beginning of the 1960's, it has been the increasing practice among states, based on claims by the Third World and as expressed in United

Nations resolutions, to consider manifestations of people's right to šelf-determination as an international event. Insurgents are also bound by International humanitarian law. The details of the application of the law are widely known.

VI. State practices indicate that national liberation movements are legitimate unlike international crimes-naked terrorism and the other heinous crimes. UN resolutions passed by the General Assembly, Security Council, International Court of Justice and several UN committees make it abundantly clear that legitimate movements are not terrorism *per se* and not mere, internal security matters. Large number of states after 1945 have emanated in this process.

VII. In compliance with the current development of International Law, the state of India ought deter itself from committing extrajudicial executions, more particularly, in the NSGT — the NE region.

VIII. The use of force is not only governed by the humanitarian laws and state practices, but also by other principles, like 'Basic Principles on the use of Force and Firearms by Law Enforcement Officials.'[25] India lacks the international legal capacity, under general international law, to use force against legitimate national liberation movements. India had consistently and religiously followed the stated position in the case of other national liberation movements elsewhere in the world.

IX. Since the crystallization of International criminal law jurisdiction in Tokyo and Nuremberg war crime tribunals and of the UN jurisdiction in Yugoslav and Rwanda tribunals in the recent years, crimes committed against a race or, ethnic cleansing or, crimes committed against humanity are subject to prosecution, trial and punishment. Protection of civilian life and property is taken more seriously in armed conflict-situation, and it is non-derogable.

X. The International Criminal Court since 2002 has come to exist and is a reality. In 2006, the ICC has investigated into and prosecuted offenders from Sudan and Uganda; the heinous criminals are being taken to task. The Government of India is under obligation to amend its criminal laws in order to fix individual criminal responsibility[26] of persons of India — be he an ordinary citizen or the prime minister or, the chief of the army staff — for commission of heinous crimes and may adopt the ICC Rome Treaty, 1998 forthwith. Heinous criminals-government officials, members of the security forces, guerrillas or soldier — could be prosecuted by the ICC, if the union government of India is honest enough to deal with them.

The government evades the ICC prosecution by not being a party as yet to the Rome Treaty, 1998 on the one hand and on the other hand, retains the old set of national criminal law without incorporating the four heinous crimes as stipulated by the Rome Treaty, 1988 thereby promoting impunity and immunity of heinous offenders, who had committed heinous crimes in the NE region for half a century.

As discussed above, the state has the responsibility and obligation to honour and comply with the internal and international human-rights standards, it has established or accepted through instrumentalities like the multilateral treaties etc, in all shifting circumstances. The insurgents are also under certain set of obligations, unless they choose to be terrorists, to protect civilian life and property; they have to declare that they abide by the minimal principles of the Geneva Conventions in this regard. It is difficult to identify NSA or, NLMs, which officially undertake, without prejudice to their political status, before the world community, their international obligations to comply with humanitarian laws. The PLA [People's Liberation Army of the RPF] of Manipur[27] in 1997 had signed Common article 3 of the Geneva Conventions at Geneva and, others are reportedly yet to sign the instrument..

However, the NSA or NLMs lack the compulsory state obligation as long as they do not constitute recognized state and become a member of the United Nations. In this sense, their obligations are more narrowed and limited than what the state had to comply with and to periodically report compliance to the comity of nations. The insurgents could demonstrate their sense of responsibility by complying with Common article 3 of the Geneva Conventions, 1949. The compliance of Common article 3, in no way, affects their political status whatsoever.

IV. THE REICH STATE UNDER CLOAK

Procedure Established by Law

In the contemporary world order, states attempt to comply with the international human rights standards; however, in state practice, notwithstanding the constitutional commitments, states deviate from the accepted track and indulge in state repression which could be inconveniently comparable to those of the Third Reich in Europe. The paper rights ensure human rights, whereas the state agencies covertly or overtly operate in later-acquired NSGT in the North-Eastern region, in ways which only the Third Reich agencies might have performed in trying circumstances for reasons of the state.

As the Indian state in practice, posed like the Third Reich in her relations with the NSGT in the aforesaid region, the civil society and the NSA or NLMs had been left with no other option than fighting back with military means or the tools of insurgency. The insurgency had proliferated because of the state repression.

The protection of life and liberty of a person including a citizen is a sacrosanct commitment of article 21 of the constitution of India which states:

> "No person shall be deprived of his life or personal liberty except according to procedure established by law."

The provision intrinsically is not an enabling law, but a disabling law. It can not and should not be construed so as to mean that one's life should be taken away, by state by simply enacting a law. A larger bench of the apex court should — it is deeply felt — review, therefore, the 27 November, 1997 judgement that extremely laboriously and notoriously *a la* a Third Reich tribunal, upheld the extra-judicial execution law of 1958.

The jurists of the affected region had perceived in a different way — had they been in the bench of the apex court, they could have unanimously scrapped the black statute at one go long back in 1980s at the time the case had been admitted without waiting for more state repression, by the apex court, as the black statute failed miserably the reasonableness test, and failed far short of India's national and international human rights obligations to terminate extrajudicial executions of Indian citizens in the NSGT of the region. The sharp difference which could be drawn between an enabling law and a disabling law can be best understood only by considering the fall out on the embedded and inbuilt paradigm of justice — the basic foundation in the constitution.

The 'procedure established by law' has been misconstrued by the wings of the state as one of the easiest ways and methods to commit gross injustice and even genocide against an alien race in NSGT. The 27 November, 1997 apex court ruling is henceforth, untenable as it has been absolutely incompatible with the accepted standards of human rights. Legality has been made the respectable mask and the cloak of embedded racial injustice in the region for half a century and the apex court merely endorsed the legality and its hidden injustice at one stroke. An exemplary counterpart is seen in the Third Reich, which has taken several millions of human lives as tuition-fee for teaching the humanity at large that one can establish such a procedure under law, and constitutionally wipe out a people (race), you dislike for absurd reasons and misspelt patriotism. The legality of the Third Reich laws is examined below because of its intellectual relevance to the region.

We learnt after paying a hefty tuition-fee after the Third Reich experiences that all the constitutional and legal acts should pass through a test of their intrinsic compatibility with the basic tenets of administering profound justice, fairness and reasonableness to the civil society. Not so long ago, the USA bought and cut off colored people as they do to the vegetables under legality upheld by the honourable or dishonourable American white supreme court, and the same was repeated in apartheid regime in South Africa under 'procedure established by law'. So did Idi Amin's or Saddam Hussein's procedure established by law. The 'procedure established by law' of these regimes had been condemned unto the last man by the civilized world. Injustice had been deeply embedded in the apparently harmless term — procedure established by law — which has been the graveyard of several uncomfortable and disposable souls.

Similarly, the parliament of India with unequal and unfair representation of the people of the NE region had enacted in 1958, the extrajudicial execution law — the AFSPA according to the 'procedure established by law', in order to give additional empowerment to the security forces to arbitrarily commit extra-judicial murders by shooting down, a race of people, who have recently joined the Indian mainstream as 'distinct people' of NSGT (Non-Self-Governing Territories). The Indian parliament has never been represented equally by all the nations and nationalities, and this inbuilt racial structure empowers dominant nations to liquidate smaller and tiny nations in the republic under the cloak of legality and assumed legitimacy. The constitutionalists ignore the fact for their own concealed and unarticulated hegemonic reasons. The cloak calls for lifting the veil as being discussed below.

Ridiculously, the Third Reich in the civilized Europe had enacted lawfully the Nuremberg laws of September 15, 1936, Reconstruction of Law, January 30, 1934 and had witnessed Emergency Presidential Decree of February 28, 1933 under article 48 of the German Constitution, the law of March 21, 1933, speciál court had been set up for trial of cases of "insidious attacks against the government." The official gazette *"Reichsgesets blatt*[28] published the lawful government orders under "AB Action" or, beautifully worded "extraordinary Pacification Action' *(Ausserordenliche Befríedigungsaktíon).* The German intelligentsia who do not subscribe to 'one people, one Reich and one faith' had been cleansed away. The Third Reich and the Indian parliament in regard to the NSGT in the NE region particularly, acted absolutely *intra vires* their respective constitutions. The apex court put its final seal of approval to the *intra vires* aspect of the execution law.

The cleansing of Germany by weeding out the undesirable hominids of some sorts had not been performed without observing constitutionality and a lawful procedure. The 'Procedure established by law' may wipe out the populace in the North-Eastern states or, the indigenous people in the region by enacting laws like the AFSPA, and the apex court totally ignored complaints since 1958, till the contemplated act has been undertaken. However, India's apex court is usually prompt to strike down, at a moments notice, incompatible statutes or executive action *suo motu* or, otherwise in the normal course. It did not happen to writ No. 550 of 1982 till 1997, until the UN Human Rights Committee literally coerced the government of India to expedite the judicial process. The parliament has repealed TADA, and not the black AFSPA. The discriminatory approaches had reinforced the legitimacy of the existing faultlines between the acquired NSGT and the metropolitan India.

The ambivalent 'procedure established by law' in the context of article 21 of the Constitution of India has undergone enormous change in the process of judicial construction. The transformation, it has undergone is crystallized below:

(1) Justice Fazal (in minority, but in saner way than the majority) in Gopalan vs. state of Madras (1950 SCR) stated that the word 'established' — suggests "certain principles of justice which inhere in every civilized systems of law" (p 180). The absence of

the word "due process" in article 21 could not lead to a possible self-righteous and arbitrary use of the procedure;

(II) The majority judgment in Maneka Gandhi vs. Union of India, A.I.R., 1978, S.C. 597 made it amply clear that whatever procedure is prescribed by the statute "cannot be arbitrary, unfair or unreasonable" (p.622). If the procedure is arbitrary or so, the court would invalidate laws which prescribed and unjust, unfair or unreasonable procedure. The procedural 'due process' has been constructed out of the silent zone of article 21;

(III) By a creative interpretation of the article 21, Justice P.N. Bhagwati enlarged the sweep of the procedure. In his words: "The principle of reasonableness, which legally as well as philosophically, is an essential element of equality or non-arbitrariness, pervades Art. 14 and omnipresence and the procedure contemplated by Art. 21 must answer the test of reasonableness in order to be in conformity with Art. 14. It must be "right and just and fair" and not arbitrary, fanciful or oppressive; otherwise it would be no procedure at all and the requirement of Art. 21 would not be satisfied."

(IV) The meaning of life under Art. 21 háve been progressively and more affirmatively interpreted by the apex court in the subsequent PIL cases. In this context, the amplitude of 'reasonableness' is widened to the extent of saving the life from arbitrary deprivation, and statutes forestall the slightest tinge of arbitrariness even in the common sense.

(V) The "Human Rights Jurisprudence", which all the agencies of the government subscribe to, by virtue

> of the International Bill of Rights and *Jus Cogens* blatantly censures extra-judicial executions and other brutalities, committed by the state. The apex court of India has, however, overlooked the inextricably and inherently unreasonable and arbitrary aspect of the state permitting extrajudicial executions in the NE region, and miraculously upheld the discriminatory law for extrajudicial execution — the AFSPA — as a good law.

The report has re-affirmed the sacrosanctity of human life in the region:

> "Inasmuch as no law has been made by the parliament under article 33 of the Constitution (as pointed out in Part II of this Report), the above-mentioned rights [*sic,* article 21 and article 19 of the Constitution] remain sacrosanct and effective even where the armed forces of the Union are deployed to restore public order and/or peace to protect a State against internal disturbance."[29]

The near permanent perpetuation of a 'lawless law' — the AFSPA — in the post-colonial period, cannot at all be justified except on the score of coercive re-colonization of a 'distinct group of people' belonging to and rooted in a distinct region, who happily remained outside the geo-political geography of India for millennia, till they had been conveniently quick-fixed to the mainland in the recent past.

The 'distinct people', more particularly — the indigenous people of the region find no other reason than considering the 'Lawless Law' as outrageously repressive. The civil society in the NE region has the feeling that the demoniacal AFSPA statute does not deserve to remain for a day longer in the statute book of a civilized legal systems. Home Minister G.B. Pant got this statute enacted as a short term measure in 1958 after a casual discussion for mere two hours only.

Historical Reasons

Immediately after Indian independence and independence of the native states in 1947, there had been turbulence in several areas including the after-acquired territories, particularly in the North-Eastern region of the country. Unlawful Activities Prevention Act, 1967 acts upon separatist forces and national liberation movements as well. The report records:

> "The ULP Act was enacted by the Parliament in 1967 to confer powers upon State authorities to deal with activities directed against the integrity and sovereignty of India"

I. In the post-colonial era, no repressive law whatsoever had ever succeeded in being instrumental towards resolving deep-structured political crisis. It could be Palestine case, Vietnam, Bangladesh or, Soviet Union in 1991 or the Indian situation under the Rowlatt Act, 1911; and, the Armed Forces Special Powers Ordinance, 1942 had rather hastened and expedited passage of Indian Independence Act, 1947, before it was actually due in June 1948.

II. The AFSPA is a crude recrudescence and revival of the British colonial statute, and it should not háve been re-enacted in the post-colonial scenario under any circumstances whatsover. AFSPA lends the best credible evidence of sustaining colonial law in a new post-colonial era. The existence of colonialism in the NE region has been testified by the law-makers themselves, who fought against the British colonialists who in their turn invoked the same ordinance to let loose state repression over the subject people.

III. The parliament of India did not fully apply its mind to the passage of this black statute for extrajudicial execution of the North-eastern people in 1958. The law which partook an emergency status had been enacted without formal declaration of emergency. Ostensibly, the statute was enacted for a brief while as it was envisaged by the home minister in the parliament and not for perpetuity as it happened thereafter for half a century. The United Nations Human Rights Committee addressed itself to this issue in 1991 and once again in July 1997. Human rights NGOs all over the world had denounced the Indian black law.

IV. When the parliament briefly discussed the purpose of invoking the law in Manipur and Naga Hills, among others, all the MPs of Manipur resisted the passage of the law. It has been thrust upon the helpless racial minority by another alien, brute and overwhelming, tyrannical majority against the vehement resistance of the miniscule racial minority. It is inherently racialist and genocidal in character from the very inception.

V. It justifies under a falše cloak of legality the state agencies to commit genocide of the NE people and thereby let loose a reign of terror which would invite armed resistance from the youths and the new generation.... Reddy report has recorded, "[when] certain members [*sic.* of the security forces] may seek to take advantage of their power and position to harass or otherwise trample upon the rights of the citizens of this country."[31]

VI. The initial objective of enacting the black law had been totally betrayed and frustrated. The statute was enacted so as to contain a small scale uprising in Naga hill district of the erstwhile state of Assam, which was just a tiny district among the large districts of Asom. After five decades of invocation of the black law, as a political fall-out, the insurgent flare-up like the proverbial prairie fire has spread over in Manipur, Assam, Nagaland, Tripura, Arunachal Pradesh, Meghalaya etc. 'The mightier the state repression, the wider is popular discontent and insurgency proliferation" — is apparently the law of nature in the new epoch.

VII. The NSGT in NE region rose against the metropolitan India for half a century. As discussed above, the republic of India has been a federated state in the sense that sovereign native states joined the union after signing instruments or treaties as per treaty laws. Certain half-baked and quack quarters or, historically misinformed academics of deeprooted racial prejudices had mistakenly raised the issue that native states were not sovereign at all notwithstanding the official statements given by Lord Mountbatten, the provisions of the Indián Independence Act, 1958 and nine supreme court verdicts on the point.

The perverted racially prejudiced scholars háve misconstrued the history of Asom, Manipur, and Tripura, among others in order to justify colonial theories. The correct legal and political position is different. The apex court verdicts would make the status of the native status quite clear and remove the unfounded postulations of the confused historians and misled political scientists.

British India was a separate entity from the sovereign native states. The Indian Supreme Court in as many as 9 verdicts since 1954 to 1993 [see - Virendra Singh vs. state of UP, AIR, 1954 SC 447 and also Raghunathrao vs.union of India, AIR 1993 SC 1267] had unambiguously laid down the verdicts that native states had been completely sovereign and independent in 1947.

The 1993 Supreme Court verdict is — *"On the commencement of the Indián Independence Act, 1947, British Paramountcy lapsed and the Indian States [sic.states including Manipur and Tripura] became completely sovereign and independent'* [emphasis added]. They conceal this historical truth for their own purposes. Native sovereign states joined or were forced to join the Indian union after signing two international treaties — the Standstill agreement, 1947 and the Instrument of Accession. Reputed Indián intellectuals refuse to acknowledge the existence of these two treaties in their critical or dishonest writings.

Hence, Indian union had been a federated state. The fabricated white academic lies and compounded multi -media racialist campaign launched against the indigenous people had misled the parliament and the state forces were indoctrinated to a considerable extent, to hate the native people of the recently acquired region.

VIII. The over all cost-benefit of the passage and invocation of the black law is counter-productive. It had already cost not less than 80,000 crore rupees of poor tax payer's money, while the starving millions of Indians need a square meal from this drained out money. In the list of HDI in 1999, India stands as the 134th in terms of human development in the world, because of this obsession. The position is not better in 2006. The arms race has also been flagged off on 11th May 1998 in South Asia with 5 nuclear weapons test inaugurated by Government of India thereby militarizing South Asia on an unprecedented scale.

IX. The NHRC of India — the apex statutory commission has recommended the repeal of AFSPA in 1997 by way of impleading in the 1997 apex court hearing. The Government of India fails to honour the impartial NHRC recommendation. The recommendation of impartial body like the NHRC is supposedly more authoritative than that of prime minister's committee, which also recommended the repeal of the lawless law for extrajudicial executions.

V. NON-COMPLIANCE WITH ARTS. 2 AND 4 OF ICCPR

The binding obligations of government of India towards the ICCPR, 1966 arises out of its signature given to and ratification of the ICCPR in 1979. The binding article 2 of the ICCPR provides, "1. Each State Party *(sic.India)* to the present Covenant undertakes to respect and to ensure to all individuals within its territory and subject to its jurisdiction the rights recognized in the present Covenant (sic. ICCPR),...".The binding obligation has not been complied with by the government of India. A brief assessment of the non-compliance of the ICCPR by the government of India is made below. Reddy report has not articulated the binding obligations of the government to the human rights treaties.

I. The declaration of disturbed area by the union government has not been guided by obvious, objective criteria. The whole exercise has been arbitrary since de facto emergency had been imposed without formal promulgation of any form of public emergency. The government of India has blatantly violated article 4, 6, 9 etc. of the ICCPR, 1966 to which it is a party. The article 4 of the ICCPR which is binding to the government of India is furnished as follows:

Article 4 [2]: "No derogation from articles 6,7,8(paragraphs l and 2), 11, 15, 16 and 18 may be made under this provision."

The right — non-derogable — even during the extreme form of public emergency, when the life of a nation is being threatened is provided by article 6 of the ICCPR which is binding to the government of India and by judicious construction, to the Supreme Court of India as well.

Article 6 [l} -"Every human being has the inherent right to life. This right shall be protected by law. No one shall be deprived of his life." The parliament of India and the apex court of India has blatantly violated article 6 and article 4 of the ICCPR, in the same way as international treaties had been cast aside by the Third Reich off late in the history. The blatant violation of human rights by the state agencies for half a century in Manipur and the NE region resulted to gross transgression of the human rights standards viz., Extrajudicial killing[32], Enforced disappearance[33], Illegal detention and harassments. p.85], Rape and sodomy [p. 86-89] and Torture [p.90-104], Report on Human Rights violations in Manipur, Committee on Human Rights, COHR, Manipur]

The Amnesty reports furnished in the last three decades or so, also corroborate the innumerable crimes committed by the state forces in Manipur and the NE region for half a century. [see all reports of Amnesty International for decades].Secret killings of as many as two hundred Assamese in the recent past have been committed by state agencies and a commission of inquiry has been set up in 2006 to find out the truth.

II. The maintenance of the public order and tranquillity is within the ambit of the Cr.P.C. Section 129 of Cr.P.C. provides for the dispersal of assembly by use of civil force; Section 130 is for the use of armed forces to disperse assembly and provides for use of armed forces to disperse assembly and it provides for power of certain armed forces officers to disperse assembly. The existing fundamental law of the land along with innumerable national security and preventive detention laws are adequate enough to mobilize armed forces in bringing peace and tranquility in the civil order. The AFSPA is an additional, but highly repressive and oppressive empowerment of the forces. The report however, observes:

"In situations of the latter kind, the provisions of the Criminal Procedure Code would not be adequate. A permanent legal provision would be required..."[34]

III. It blatantly violates the internal and international standards of human rights, as enunciated above and universally agreed upon. It negates India's conviction and national commitment.

IV. Section 4(a), (b), (c), (d), of the black law acts apparently in direct transgression upon articles

21 and 22 of the Constitution. The power to 'fire upon' to the extent of causing death given to the lowest rung of NCO on the slightest suspicion i.e. the power to commit extra-judicial execution is not only arbitrary, unjust, unfair, but is also a naked legitimization of outright extrajudicial murder. No civilized jurisprudence would justify this additional empowerment, given to the forces to kill citizens.

The apex court by its 27 November, 1997 judgment failed to give ample judicial reason to route the criticism of the powers so exercised under the black law. It has in just one or, two pages very feebly and vulnerably upheld section 4 of the Statute. It has run short of juristic ammunition, while defending—(a) the unproclaimed public emergency by overlooking the emergency provisions of the Constitution of Indiia (b) the racialist and discriminatory law for the subjugation of the NE people, and (c) extrajudicial execution in perpetuity, of the people of the NSGT in direct contravention of the ICCPR, 1966, general international law, and *Jus Cogens*.

V. The apex court judgment commands respectability and bindingness according to article 141 of the Constitution. The Delhi High Court judgment — Indrajit Barua vs. State of Assam (AIR 1983, Delhi 513) had the least bearing with article 141. The Supreme Court has disposed of the writ petition nos. 5328 of 1980, 550 of 1982 and 9229 and 9230 of 1982, which challenged the constitutionality of impugned black statute, on November 27, 1997 after long seventeen years of receiving the petition in 1980. The Supreme Court had been calculatively indifferent to the extrajudicial execution of the people of the North-eastern civil society.

After accepting a set of guidelines to be followed at the time of enforcing the law, the apex court has upheld the validity of the Armed Forces (Special Powers) Act, 1958, the repeal of which has also been recommended in the process of impleading, by the Chairman of the National Human Rights Commission in 1996-97. The constitutional bench, headed by Chief Justice, J. S Verma, in its 60 page judgment observed that the parliament could enact the impugned statute, under power conferred under article 248 read with list 1 entry 2, entry 97 and entry 2A, inserted after the 42nd Constitutional amendment.

The verdict borders on the extreme edge of technical formalism of the crudest positivist kind, which is totally devoid of the public justice, as accepted at this stage of our civilization. Till a full bench of the apex court (13 judges or so) takes a review of the 1997 decision, the positivist verdict stands in justification for a draconian law legitimizing extrajudicial executions. The Supreme Court in spirit had upheld a statute comparable to that of a Nazi statute in post-colonial republic of India.

The PUDR rightly observed, "The court refused to go into the actual working of the Act and deemed it irrelevant for purposes of deciding its constitutionality, and the basic fact that the Constitution does not envisage long term deployment of the armed forces in civilian areas has been meticulously overlooked..."

VI. The apex court did not apply its mind to the relevance of humanitarian laws to the conflict —

situation in the NE region. It has deliberately overlooked India's treaty laws like the ICCPR, 1966.

International Standards

All the black laws — particularly, the AFSPA, 1958 — enacted by the parliament of India are found to be manifestly incompatible with the international standard accepted by the government of India, for the following reasons:

I. The United Nations Human Rights Committee in 1991 found section 4 of the AFSPA and other sections too, to be incompatible with articles 6, 9, and 14 of the International Covenant on Civil and Political Rights, 1966, the compliance of which has become union government's binding obligation, following India's ratification of the Covenant on 10 April, 1979; the incompatibility has not yet been rectified by the union government; 'Right to life' cannot be violated even when the life of a nation like India is being threatened during war. The union government has blatantly violated article 4 of the ICCPR for 50 years.

II. The UN Human Rights Committee in 1997[35] had observed the following for necessary compliance by the govemment of India, and also for reporting on the compliance in 2001 when the 4th periodic report of India was due, i.e. 5 years back from the present:

"18. The committee. ... Hopes that its[AFSPA] provisions will also be examined for their compatibility with the Covenant.

19. The Committee regrets that some parts of India háve remained subject to declaration as disturbed areas for many years — for example the Armed Forces (Special Powers) Act has been applied throughout Manipur since

1980 and in some areas of that state for much longer-, and that in these areas the State party is in effect using emergency powers without resorting to article 4, para 3 of the Covenant.

21.—It urges that judicial enquiries be mandatory in all cases of death at the hands of the security and armed forces and that the judges in such enquiries including those under the Commission of Enquiry Act of 1952, be empowered to direct prosecution of security and armed forces personnel.

22. The Committee ... recommends that the National Human Rights Committee be authorized to investigate all allegations of violations by agents of State.

23.—, it [the HR committee] recommends: a the early enactment of legislation for mandatory judicial enquiry into cases of disappearances and death, ill-treatment or rape in police custody.

35. The Committee... requests that, its next periodic report due on 31 December, 2001, should contain material which responds to all these Concluding Observations...."The government of India has not paid sufficient attention to these recommendations and defers the submission of the 4th report to the UN Human Rights Committee for 5 years, possibly to give along rope to the national institutions so as to continue extra-judicial executions and enjoy impunity for a longer period during the period of non-submission of the report. The political leadership has been apparently under pressure from the bureaucracy, which equates their brand of nationalism with extrajudicial executions with absolute impunity.

III. The enlightened opinion passes strictures on the violation of human rights by the state with the instrumentality of black laws. The Amnesty International in 1993 had recommended that the government should review the black law and incorporate the minimum safeguards, as provided in the relevant articles of the covenant. The Amnesty had further recommended in April 1997 that the

Government of India should "review the Armed Forces (Special Powers) Act to ensure that there are strict legal limitations on the use of force and firearms by law enforcement officials", and "remove the requirement of sanction for the prosecution of police or armed forces personnel under section 7 of the Armed Forces (Spacial Powers) Act."

IV. Reputed human rights organizations in India had submitted memoranda to the National Human Rights Commission by censuring and denouncing sections 3, 4 and 5 of the AFSPA, which háve been instrumental in the gross violations of human rights.

V. The UNHRC in 1997 has recommended that the government of India should remove restrictions, given by article 19 of the 1993 Human Rights Act.

VI. Prevention of Terrorism (Additional Powers) Act 1967 and also the 1989 Act had been inappropriately cited as reference point of United Kingdom.

But they are temporary measures unlike the perpetual AFSPA. In United Kingdom, the anti-terrorist Act of 1989 — now, 1996 has been invariably followed by a political package like the 'Downing Street Declaration' (Anglo-Irish), December 15, 1994 prescribing right of the Irish people to Šelf-determination and 10th April Belfast Agreement 1998. The 1998 Belfast agreement had been worked out by the active involvement of a third party — the USA president and two prime ministers. These basic parameters are conveniently overlooked by the legislators.

In British India also, the demoniacal Armed Forces (Special Powers) Ordinance 1942 was not enacted without itself being followed by the complementary, all healing Indián Independence Act, 1947. The Brits are committed to relinquishing Northern Ireland in phases and after taking people's wishes into consideration, by virtue of the 1998 Agreement. The British precedent has been insufficiently and inappropriately cited by the Indian administration and the Law Commission of India. Indian legislators would cite the most offensive pieces of legislation only and discard healing legislations which are inextricable from the former.

VII. The Non-Self-Governing-Territories — NSGT in North-Eastern region are in need of a popular consultation in more or less the same fashion as it had been arranged in the case of East Timor on 30 August, 1999. The political status calls for re-enunciation in order to pave way for a lasting, durable and just solution in the NE region. The nightmare has been too long for the NE people and a dawn is yet to descend on them.

VI. TASK AHEAD

The gross human rights violations in the North-Eastern states of India háve been fully documented by human rights NGOs in India. The Amnesty International observes that the AFSPA 1958 empowers the government to make '*de facto* derogation from non-derogable covenant rights', and it has recurrently urged upon the UNHRC to examine the factum of this derogation.

By criticizing the black law — AFSPA 1958 and the licence to shoot and kill and citizens merely on suspicion, SHRDC observes, "These provisions give a broad licence to extra-judicially execute" innocent and suspected persons under the disguise of maintaining law and order. It violates every norm of civilized society. The juridical conscience in the apex court and elsewhere legitimized extra-judicial massacres in blatant disregard of the enlightened world public opinion against extrajudicial executions and tortures..

The UN Human Rights Committee while showing deep concern at the state's continuing reliance on the AFSPA, the Public Safety Act and National Security Act, which are incompatible with Article 6, 7, 9 and 14 of the Covenant had recommended in 1997 that the insurgency problems which are essentially political in character be resolved with means that are compatible with the Covenant. Reacting against clause 19 of the Protection of Human Rights Act 1993, the UNHRC had also recommended that "these restrictions be removed and that the National Human Rights Commission be authorized to investigate all allegations of violations by agents of the State." The government of India continues to uphold illegitimate and unlawful derogation of the ICCPR, 1966.

The union government of India has already considered the insurgency as a political question, and initiated unconditional political dialogue with a section of hill insurgents since August 1997; but it left out other effective and equally viable insurgent groups from the political dialogue on the chronic political questions. The Peoples Consultative Committee [PCG] of Asom had in 2006 entered into preliminary round of talks with the government of India in order to facilitate talks in between the NSA or National Liberation Movement in Asom and the union government on the demands of sovereignty of Asom and economic issues as well. The union government has evaded the dialogue on the sovereignty of Asom and harps on peripheral issues.

The United Nations Human Rights Committee in its

recommendations had also noted that the issue is simply political and calls for political solution. The very fact of holding political negotiation between the union government and the insurgent group on the initiative of the former has disapproved the widely circulated administrative misnomer in treating the political questions as ordinary law and order problem. The polemic is virtually self-contradictory.

The Supreme Court bench, headed by Chief Justice J.S. Verma heard seven petitions challenging the constitutionality of the impugned Armed Forces (Special Powers) Act, 1958, the first of which has been filed by the Manipur Human Rights Forum in October 1980. The bench upheld the law that interferes with the deep-rooted political question, India's Defence Minister, George Fernandez, however, calls for repeal of the black law of 1958 during his tenure. Prime Minister Manmohan Singh has expressed his intention in December middle 2006 to scrap the black law if the parties could reach at a consensus on the repeal issue. The continuance of the black law gives a fillip to the insurgents and rebels who had waited for clear evidence of colonial repression from the Indian state.

The PUDR report, May 1998 — 'An lllusion of Justice-Supreme Court Judgement on the Armed Forces [Special Powers) Act' had criticized the supreme court verdict on the AFSPA. It records, "The court refused to go into the actual working of the Act and deemed it irrelevant for purposes of deciding its constitutionality."[36]

Justice Reddy report has found little comfort with the Supreme Court judgement on AFSPA. It has observed, "It is true that the Hon'ble Supreme Court has upheld its constitutional validity but that circumstance is not an endorsement of the desirability or advisability of the Act....The Court does not — it is not supposed to pronounce upon the wisdom or necessity of such an enactment."[37] It appears that the Supreme Court had acted more on legitimization of extrajudicial executions of genocidal nature than upholding the firmly established constitutional values on sanctity of human life in difficult times, and the international rule of law on human rights which háve direct bearing with the Indian laws and obligations.

After prolonged mass movements in Manipur state of the country, in the wake of gang rape and extrajudicial execution of Miss Thangjam Manorama by the 17th Assam Rifles on the fateful 11 July 2004, for the immediate repeal of the infamous AFSPA which had been mercilessly invoked for half a century in the entire North-East region, the prime minister admitted the inhumane nature of the black law in 2004, and has constituted a five-member committee under the chairmanship of Justice B.P. Jeevan Reddy, who submitted the report in June 2005 to the prime minister for necessary action. The prime minister refrained from taking action on the report for a long time.

After conducting public hearings in New Delhi and the North-Eastern states barring the statutory National Human Rights Commission of India, Reddy committee has chalked out it options before material recommendations háve been made.

They are — "The Committee finds that there are four options available for it to adopt viz.,

(a) to recommend the repeal of the Armed Forces (Special Powers) Act, 1958;

(b) to recommend that the present Act should continue as it obtains today or with such amendments as may be found appropriate;

(c) in case the repeal of the Armed Forces [Special Powers) Act is recommended, to recommend that it should be replaced by an appropriate legislation;

(d) in case of recommendation of repeal of the Act, to recommend insertion of appropriate provisions in an existing/cognate enactment.[38]

The Report (Jeevan Reddy Committee report) made two major recommendations-firstly, for total repeal of the AFSPA, 1958 and secondly, for incorporation of some of the provisions of the black law in the Unlawful Activities (Prevention) Act, 1967 as amended in 2004.

It has observed, the Act, for whatever reason, has become a symbol of oppression, an object of hate and an instrument of discrimination and highhandedness." The main recommendation is—

> "(a) the armed Forces (Special Powers) Act, 1958 should be repealed. Therefore, recommending the continuation of the present Act, with or without amendments, does not arisc."[39]

However, the report has encouraged backdoor-entry or colorable legislation of some of the bad provisions of the otherwise would be repealed statute in another existing statute by making a departure from the committee's firm stand against inhumane provisions. The Report states:

> "(b) The Committee is also of the firm view that it would be more appropriate to recommend insertion of appropriate provisions in the Unlawful Activities (Prevention) Act, 1967(as amended in the year 2004) —Which is a cognate enactment as pointed out in Chapter III Part II of this Report instead of suggesting a new piece of legislation."[40]

Reddy report suggests, among others, for incorporation in the ULAPA, 2002 the following:

"(5)(b): In the course of undertaking operations mentioned in (a) above, any officer not below the rank of a non-commissioned officer, may, if it is necessary, in his judgement for an effective conduct of operations, use force or fire upon, after giving due warning, an individual or a group of individuals unlawfully carrying or in possession of or is reasonably suspected of being in unlawful possession of the articles mentioned in Section 15 of this Act."[41]

The Report suggests:

"Section 40-E : The Armed Forces [Special Powers) Act, 1958 is repealed herewith."[42] [emphasis added]

The report has been silent on the preponderant issues relating to the prevention of extrajudicial executions and termination of impunity of the offenders. The studied, possibly calculated silence would encourage the law-makers and law interpreters to take complete liberties with the life of citizens. Immediately after receipt of the report, the army reacted in 2006 strongly — by implication that they are in dire need of powers to commit extrajudicial executions and immunity for the crimes, they would like to commit. The state has encouraged the forces to identity nationalism with extrajudicial executions and absolute immunity. By the human rights standard, these arguments are untenable.

Before tabling the report to the parliament, in an apparent breach of the privilege of the house, the government submitted the report to its military muscle — the Indián army in 2006. The chief of the army General J.J. Singh asked for immunity of the soldiers from judicial scrutiny of alleged crimes committed by the members of the forces. He has stated: "We cannot fight with both hands tied behind our backs. We need some sort of immunity for our soldiers from court cases.". The world community stands as one man to terminal impunity of heinous criminals, and the rule of law evolved by human civilization does not deserve termination at the hands of powerful terminators or institutions.

New Delhi summit of civil society organizations held at the Press Club on 17 October, 2005 in presence of large number of print media of the country, which meticulously and very systematically like the Goebbel's media blacked out the proceedings from professional reporting for extraneous reasons under the conventional cloak of press liberty or whatever they had in their mind, has urged upon the union government of India to forthwith scrap the black law — AFSPA, 1958, and also to see subsequently that black norms recommending extrajudicial executions, torture and according impunity to extrajudicial executioners are not incorporated in any other existing law. Subsequently thereafter, several rallies, conferences and meeting of the opposition parties of the country had urged upon the government to repeal the black statute. Some of the speakers and jurists alerted that military rule should not be imposed all over the country subsequently after the repeal of the black law.

The Repeal Discourse

The draconian law — AFSPA — 1958 — that blatantly violates the vital provisions of the International covenants to which India is a party, infringes upon the basic tenets of civilized norms and 'Rule of Law' for the last half a century does not deserve a respectable space in the statute. Nobel laureate Shirin Ibadi has vowed on November 28, 2006 in New Delhi that she would take up the AFSPA repeal issue to the UN High Commissioner for Human Rights, the recently established UN Human Rights Council and all the international fora and also to the Speaker of

Indian Loka Sabha, among others, for stopping the half a century long state repression.[44]

The Iranian Nobel laureate spoke to the HINDU daily.[45] that the Indian parliament, the courts and the armed forces should be responsible if Irom Sharmila who had been fast unto death for six years dies. The Speaker of the Lok Sabha and all the opposition parties by following the footsteps of the Nobel laureate espoused the repeal of the black law in December, 2006. The prime minister also has changed his mindset, and expressed his intent to repeal the statute.

The discourse pattern unfolds into two planes — one, deeply rooted in the infantile obsession or, patriotic romanticism, which ought not to be circumscribed by a rights regime whatever and — another, evolved by the super-eminent civilizational values that place human security and the accepted human rights standards above all the localized political expediencies. Territoriality, right of the people to self-determination, and use of force are not uncontested spaces for a fruitful and understandable argumentation in the contemporary world. The preponderance of the argumentation could be placed somewhere in the possible confluence or, overlapping space of the two contending propositions. Legality is no longer considered sacrosanct, as it could be a cloak of unlimited heinous crimes committed by a state against vulnerable population groups, and legitimization could also be a suspect in different contexts.

It is ironical that on occasions, the judiciary finds itself a convenient instrument or unproclaimed prisoner of conscience of a leviathan state in the process of legalizing the illegality and legitimizing the injustice. India is not an exception, and the apex court verdict in 1997 is not the best verdict a post-Nazi, informed judiciary could deliver at a time, when extrajudicial executions continued for decades against a distinct population or people in the country. History will not easily erase out what wrongs had been conscientiously committed by all the national institutions with tacit understanding in collectivity.

The new world order has invariably, through bitter human experiences and scourges of two world wars, has laid down certain human rights benchmarks from which deviations and departures are considered as incompatible with the civilization, humanity has painfully evolved and nurtured. Immunity and impunity, once considered to be the necessary evil are substituted by individual responsibility, irrespective of the state sovereignty. The lawless law — the AFSPA, denounced by the enlightened world opinion and jurists for several decades has also to be assessed by the standard-setting process of the human rights regime — national or otherwise, international whatever. The national institutions which laboured hard to defend the heinous crimes, and defended the immunity and impunity of the extrajudicial killers in the uniform, under the cloak of nationalism and far-fetched legality, have not best performed their job in the name of justice and humanity, and henceforth, they háve to remain a stigma on humanity.

The deep-structured political and nationality questions that characterize the turmoil in the North-Eastern states with a population of 40 million for half a century, deserve political attention and resolution. Notwithstanding the changing political dynamics and fluidity in the discourse-pattern, the fact remains that the global human rights standard had been consistently and systematically violated by the union government of India in a situation of *de facto* unproclaimed emergency. It is time that the government of India repeals immediately the infamous AFSPA and, in due course of time, signs the ICC Rome Treaty, 1998 and terminates impunity enjoyed for half a century by the state security forces or civil administration whatever in this part of the world.

REFERENCES

1. All the well known documents are not documented in this article to save space. For details, see books by the author viz., 1] *Human Rights,* Omsons, ND, 1994 ed., 2] *Human Rights in the New Millennium,* Manas, ND, 2000, 3] *Human Rights-Current Issues,* Omsons, ND, 2004, 4] *International Human Rights,* vol. I,II,III, ND, 2005, among others.

   Cf. N. Sanajaoba, *A Critique of Armed Forces (Special Powers) Act, 1958* J Department of Law, GU, May, 1998—see detail references at the endnotes. For elaborate examination of the author's critique of the AFSPA among others, see 398 insertions of Naorem Sanajaoba in GOOGLE search or, 261 insertions in yahoo Isearch. Cf. Asian Centre for Human Rights, The AFSPA: Lawless Law Enforcement According to the Law ?, January, 2005.
2. Justice Jeevan Reddy Report, 2005-downloaded from the HINDU daily paper, Page numbers are followed from the HINDU download, since the GOI has not released the report in public except to the armed forces-hereafter report only.
3. *Ibid.,* p. 5.
4. See Manorama Timeline in < www.e-pao.net> for all details and mass uprisings in Manipur in 2004. Manipur people had undertaken continuous mass movements under the leadership of the APUNBA LUP from July 2004 for several months and during the movements, Pebam Chittaranjan self-immolated himself, 5 another youts tried self-immolation, but saved. Sharmila continued her fast unto death since 2000, Manipuri mothers undressed before the Assam Rifles gate inviting them to rape the Manipuri women and hundreds of youths, students had been brutally tortured by the forces;

new generation lost classes and education. At a point of time, the PM proclaimed the act to be inhumane.

5. see Sharmila Timeline in<www,e-pao.net> for all details for the last years of her fast unto death—the first ever in human history.
6. Report p. 75.
7. *Ibid.*, p. 74.
8. *Ibid.*, p. 62.
9. *Ibid.*, p. 64.
10. *lbid.*, p. 10.
11. Lok Sabha Debates second series, volume XVIII, 1958, [1 lth August to 22nd August, 1958] Lok Sabha Secretariat, New Delhi-LSD hereafter.
12. LSD, p. 1441.
13. *Ibid.*, p. 1447.
14. *Ibid.*, 1434.
15. *Ibid.*, p. 1426.
16. *Ibid.*, p. 1401.
17. *Ibid.*, p. 1406.
18. *Ibid.*, p. l409.
19. See Lahiri, *Annexation of Assam,* Firma KLM, Calcutta; PDM, Annexation of Manipur 1949, Imphal,1995,N. Sanajaoba, Manipur Puwaari Kunamathoishuba Chahicha, NRC, Imphal, 2006 and all the history books of the NE region whatever.
20. See A.C. Banerjee, *The Eastern Frontier of British India,* K.P. Bagchi & Co, Calcutta, 1943, pp. 335-376.
21. *Op. cit.,* PDM, pp. 7-28.
22. Op. cit Reddy report, p. 11.
23. *Ibid.*, p. 79.
24. *Ibid.*, p. 78
25. UN, Professional Training Series 5,1997 on Enforcement of Law.
26. N.Sanajaoba, ed., *A Manual of International Humanitarian Law,* Regency, ND, 2004; see his articles on ICC since 2001 and other prolific articles in law journal and mass media.
27. See website www.geocities.com RPF; 49* session of UN Human Rights sub-commission at Geneva-Declaration by the President, RPF[army-PLA] on 6th August, 1997 —"The

Revolutionary People's Front.... HEREBY DECLARE, on this day the 6th of August 1997. Its unequivocal intention to comply with all the provisions of Article 3 common to the four Geneva Conventions of August 12,1949". The NLM also urged upon the Government of India to sign and ratify the two Additional Protocols, 1977 in reciprocity; the GOI is yet to sign the two Additional Protocols. Several NLMs in the region are yet to officially comply with the mandate of 1HL, irrespective of their political status.

28. Plenty of books journals are available on the great Führer and his laws, war so on.
29. *Op. cit.,* Reddy report, p. 70s.
30. *Ibid.,* p. 29.
31. *Ibid.,* p. 73.
32. Human Rights violations in Manipur, 2005, COHR — Committee on Human Rights, Manipur, pp. 1-82.
33. *Ibid.,* pp. 83-84; See also Amnesty International reports during the last three decades; see 'Where peacekeeprs have declared war, April, 1997, National Campaign Committee Against Militarisation, New Delhi.
34. *Op. cit.* Reddy report, p. 41.
35. See ICCPR report on India-CCPR/IND/3, 1 August, 1997, Geneva.
36. *Op. cit.,* Report, p. 3.
37. *Ibid.,* p. 74.
38. *Id.*
39. *Id.*
40. *Ibid.,* p. 75.
41. *Ibid.,* p. 84.
42. *Ibid.,* p 82
43. *Telegraph* daily, Guwahati edition, 21 October, 2006.
44. *The Hindu* daily, 27 November, 2006, p. 12.
45. *The Hindu* daily, 29 November, 2006, p. 3.

Document

Report of the Committee to Review the Armed Forces (Special Powers) Act, 1958*

PART-IV: RECOMMENDATIONS

The Committee has carefully considered the various views, opinions and suggestions put forward by the representatives of organisations and individuals who appeared before it as also the presentations and representations made by the concerned departments of the governments, security agencies and other organisations and individuals.

2. While devising a solution to the problem referred to the Committee, it has to bear in mind the following three basic conditions, viz.,

ONE - The security of the nation, which is of paramount importance. Security of, the nation involves security of the States as well. The very first entry in the Union List In the Seventh Schedule to the Constitution speaks of defence of India and every part thereof which means and implies that it is the power and obligation of the President, the Parliament and the Union Government to ensure the defence of India and of every part there of. Though purporting to be a division of legislative powers between the Union and the States, the Seventh Schedule to the Constitution, it is well accepted, does represent the division of powers between the Union and the States. £even if a law is not made under and with reference to a particular entry / legislative head, the executive power would still be available under that

*Acknowledgements to the *Hindu* daily.

entry. Lists-I and II set out the legislative heads / powers of the Union and the States respectively while List-III sets out the legislative heads, with reference to which both the Parliament and the State Legislatures can make laws, subject, of course, to the rule of parliamentary predominance recognised by Article 254. For ensuring the defence of India and of its every part, the Parliament can make such law and / or the Union government can take such executive action, as may be found necessary or proper. Some of the ways in which the Union government performs the said obligation are mentioned in Articles 352 to 356, (as pointed out in Chapter II of Part II of this Report. Article 355, which places an obligation upon the Union to protect every State against external aggression and internal disturbance and also to ensure that the Government of every State is carried on in accordance with the provisions of this Constitution, has also been referred to at some length in the said part of this Report). It is necessary to clarify that the Constitution does not contemplate that the obligation to protect the States in the Union shall be carried out by the Union Government only by invoking Article 352 (external aggression or internal rebellion) or Article 356 (to ensure that the government of every State is carried on in accordance with the provisions of the Constitution); the said obligation can be performed in such manner as may be found appropriate, without of course violating the spirit and latter of the Constitution.

Now, coming to Article 355; it may be reiterated that the obligation created by Article 355 includes the duty to protect every State against internal disturbance as well. "Internal disturbance", as pointed in Part II of this Report, represent a very serious, large scale and sustained chaotic conditions spread over a large area of the State. It is no doubt the power and obligation of the state Government to maintain public order as is evident from Entry 1 of State list in the Seventh Schedule to the Constitution. However, the said entry read with Entry 2A of the Union List means that (a) where the State Government finds that it is not able to maintain public order and it is of the opinion that the aid of the armed forces / forces under the control of the Union is necessary for maintaining or restoring the public order, it can request the Union Government to send the armed forces to maintain and restore the public order; (b) even where the State Government does not so request but the Union Government is satisfied that for protecting the State from "internal disturbance" i.e. to save it from domestic chaos or internal commotion, it is necessary' to deploy armed forces of the Union, it can do so under Art.355.

TWO - It is equally the duty of the Union and the States to not only respect the fundamental rights conferred upon the citizens of India by Part III and other provisions of the Constitution; they are also under an obligation to ensure the conditions wherein the citizens can enjoy and avail of the fundamental and other rights available to the citizens. In particular, Article 21 of the Constitution expressly declares that no person shall be deprived of his life or personal liberty except in accordance with the procedure established by law. Article 14 in Part III of the Constitution ensures to its citizens equality before law and equal protection of laws within the territory of India which means that no citizen or group of citizens shall be discriminated vis-a-vis any other citizen of group of citizens. Article 19 confers upon the citizens six valuable freedoms viz., freedom of speech and expression; freedom to assemble peacefully and without arms; freedom to form associations or unions; freedom to move freely throughout the territory of India freedom to reside and settle in any part of the territory of India and the freedom to practise any profession or to carry on any occupation, trade or business subject or course to such reasonable restrictions thereon as may be placed by a law made by the Parliament or State Legislatures under clauses (2) to (6) of the said article. Clauses (1) and (2) of Article 22 confer equally valuable rights upon the citizens of India. Clause (1) declares that (19 person who is arrested shall be detained in custody without being\ informed, as soon as may be, of the grounds for such arrest nor shall he be denied the right to consult, and to be defended, by the legal practitioner of his choice. Clause '(2) declares that every person who is arrested and detained in custody shall be produced before the nearest Magistrate within a period of 24 hours excluding the time taken for journey from the place of arrest to the nearest court of the Magistrate. Inasmuch as no law has been made by Parliament under Article 33 of the Constitution (as pointed out in Part II of this Report), the above mentioned rights remain sacrosanct and effective even where the armed forces of the Union are deployed to restore public order and/or peace or to protect a State against Internal disturbance. Articles 25 to 30 ensure the freedom of religion and ensure to every religious denomination or any section thereof to manage its religious affairs; they ensure freedom of worship, right to conserve one's own culture and also confer a right upon the minorities to establish educational institutions of their choice.

THREE - The armed forces of the Union viz., the army, navy and the air force are meant to ensure the defence of the Union and all its parts. In other words, the armed forces are meant to guard our borders against any aggression by any foreign power or foreign agency, irrespective of the manner in which such aggression is perpetrated. The armed forces are trained and are equipped for this purpose. May be that in an emergency like a flood or other natural calamity, armed forces are also called in to provide relief and help the people but that is only a temporary phenomenon. The Union Government has also been creating and indeed expanding various para military forces under various enactments like the Border Security Force Act, Assam Rifles Act, Indo-Tibetan Border Police Act, CRPF Act, CISF Act and so on. The Union Government has also created what is known as "India Reserve Battalions". Though these para military forces have been created for certain specific purposes, yet, on account of the disturbed situation in certain parts of the country, the Union Government has been obliged to deploy, from time to time, these forces as well as its armed forces to redress these situations. It must be recognised, at the same time, that the deployment of armed forces or para military forces of the Union to restore public order in any part of the territory of India, or to protect a State from internal disturbance is, and ought to be, an exception and not the rule. The deployment of armed forces for the said purposes should be undertaken with great care and circumspection. Unless it is absolutely essential for the aforesaid purposes, the armed forces of the Union should not be so deployed, since too frequent a deployment, and that too for long periods of time, carries with it the danger of such forces losing their moorings and becoming, in effect, another police force, a prey to all the temptations and weaknesses such exposures involve. Such exposure for long periods of time may well lead to the brutalisation of such forces which is a danger to be particularly guarded against. This concern applies no less in the case of other armed forces of the Union as well. All this means that as soon as the public order is restored or the internal disturbance is quelled, the forces have to be withdrawn to their barracks or to their regular duties, as the case may be. This very concern and consideration underlies Sections 130 and 131 of the Code of Criminal' Proceduce, which have been referred to and dealt with in Chapter IV of Part II of this Report. These sections of the Code of Criminal Procedure make it repeatedly clear that where it is necessary to call in the army to disperse an unlawful assembly endangering public security, the armed forces so called in shall act according to the directions-of the Magistrate though the manner in which the armed forces perform the task entrusted to them lies within their discretion. Even where the armed forces are called in for meeting a more serious threat to public order or public security, or where the deployment of the armed forces is required on a fairly long-term basis, this concern remains equally valid. It has also to be ensured that the legal mechanism under which they function is sufficiently clear and specific and accords with the spirit and provisions of the Constitution as adumbrated hereinabove. While providing protection against civil or criminal proceedings in respect of the acts and deeds done by such forces while carrying out the duties entrusted to them, it is equally necessary to ensure that where they knowingly abuse or misuse their powers, they must be held accountable therefor and must be dealt with according to law applicable to them. It is not unusual that there will be some indisciplined individuals in these forces as well, but their wrong actions should not be allowed to sully the fair name of the armed forces and the para military, forces. While our armed forces are one of the most disciplined in the world situations may arise when they are deployed outside their regular duties, i.e. when they are deployed for maintaining public order or for quelling internal disturbance in a part of the territory of India, when certain members thereof may seek to take advantage of their power and position to harass or otherwise trample upon the rights of the citizens of this country. The legal mechanism should ensure that such incidents do not take place and should also ensure that adequate remedial measures do exist where such incidents do take place.

3. Bearing the above considerations in mind, we have to proceed ahead. At this juncture it would be appropriate to recall the terms of reference given to this — Committee. They read as follows:

> "Keeping in view the legitimate concerns of the people of the North-Eastern Region, the need to foster Human Rights, keeping in perspective the imperatives of security and maintenance of public order to review the provisions of' the Armed Force; (Spacial Powers) Act, 1958 as amended in 1972 and to advise the Government of India whether:
>
> (a) To amend the provisions of the Act to brlng them in consonance with the obligatlons of the Govt. towards protection of Human Rights; or
>
> (b) To replace the Act by a more humane Act.

The Committee may Interact with representatives of social groups, State Governments and concerned agencies of Central Govt./State Govt. legal experts and (individuals, as deemed necessary by the Committee in connection with the review of the Armed Forces (Spacial Powers) Act, 1958 as amended in 1972.

The Committee will meet as often as required and visit the North Eastern Region, if felt necessary."

4. The Committee finds that there are four options availab͏le for it to adopt viz.,

(a) to recommend the repeal of the Armed Forces (Spacial Powers) Act, 1958;

(b) to recommend that the present Act should continue as it obtains today or with such amendments as may be found appropriate;

(c) in case the repeal of the Armed Forces (Spacial Powers) Act, 1958 is recommended, to recommend that it should be replaced by an appropriate legislation;

(d) in case of recommendation for repeal of the -Act, to recommend insertion of appropriate provisions in an existing l /cognate enactment.

5. Keeping in view the material placed before us and *the* impressions gathered by the Committee during the course of its visits and hearings held within and outside the North-Eastern States, the Committee is of the firm view that:

(a) The Armed Forces (Spacial Powers) Act, 1958 should be repealed. Therefore, recommending the continuatlon of the, present Act, with or without amendments, does not arise. The Act is too sketchy, too bald and quite inadequate in several particulars. It is true that the Hon'ble Supreme Court has upheld its constitutional validity but that circumstance is not an endorsement of the desirability or advisability of the Act. When the constitutional validity of an enactment is challenged in a Court, the Court examines (i) whether the Act is within the legislative competence of the Legislature which enacted it and (ii) whether the enactment violates any of the provisions of the Constitution.

The Court does not — it is not supposed to pronounce

upon the wisdom or the necessity of such an enactment. It must be remembered that even while upholding its constitutional validity, the Hon'ble Court has found it fit and necessary not merely to approve the; "Dos and Don'ts" in the instructions issued by the Army Headquarters from time to time but has also added certain riders of its own viz., those contained in clauses 8, 9 and 14 to 21 in para 74 of its judgment (at pages 156 and 157 of the judgment in NAGA PEOPLES' MOVEMENT OF HUMAN RIGHTS v. UNION OF INDIA — (1998) 2 SCC 109). The Committee is of the opinion that legislative shape must be given to many of these riders. We must also mention the impression gathered by it during the course of its work viz., the Act for whatever reason, has become a symbol of oppression, an object of hate and an instrument of discrimination and high-handedness. It is highly desirable and advisable to repeal this Act altogether, without, of course, losing sight of the overwhelming desire of an overwhelming majority of the region that the Army should remain (though the Act should go). For that purpose, an appropriate legal mechanism has to be devised.

(b) The Committee is also of the firm view that it would be more appropriate to recommend insertion of appropriate provisions in the Unlawful Activities (Prevention) Act, 1967 (as amended in the year 2004) -- which is a cognate enactment as pointed out in Chapter III Part II of this Report Instead of suggesting a new piece of legislation.

6. The reasons for adopting the course of introducing requisite and appropriate provisions in the Unlawful Activities (Protection) Act are as follows:

ONE - The ULP Act defines "terrorism" In terms which encompass and cover the activities of the nature carried on by several militant/insurgent organisations in the North-east States. Use of arms and/or explosives so as to cause loss of life or property or to act against a government servant, with intent elder to threaten the unity, integrity, security or sovereignty cf India or to strike terror in the people or any section of the people in India or in any foreign country (as provided by Section 15), the kind of activity carried on by various militant / insurgent organisations in the North-east, falls withln.the four corners of Sections15. It is terrorism within the meaning of the Act.

TWO - The ULP Act not only defines 'terrorism' in expansive terms but also specifically lists some of the organizations engaged in militant / insurgent activity in Manipur, Tripura, Nagaland and Assam as terrorist organizations in the schedule appended to the Act. In other words, the Act recognizes that the activities carried on by the schedule mentioned organizations fall within the definition of 'terrorism' and 'terrorist activity' as defined by the said Act. Furthermore, as pointed out in Chapter III of Part II of this Report, the ULP Act does contemplate, by necessary Implication, the use of armed forces of the Union as well as the other para military forces under the control of the Union to fight and curb the terrorist activities in the country. It is for the said reason that It has expressly barred, in Section 49, any suit, prosecution or other legal proceedings against "any serving or retired member of the armed forces or para military forces in respect of any action taken or purported to be taken by him in good faith, in the course of any operation directed towards combating terrorism". In this sense the ULP Act, as it now obtains, does provide for deploying the armed forces or para-military forces for fighting the militant/insurgent/terrorist activity being carried on in some or all North-eastern States.* The Act is designed to curb the rrorist activities of not only the organisations mentioned in the schedule but any and every terrorist activity.

THREE - A major consequence of the proposed course would be to erase the feeling of discrimination and alienation among the people of the North-eastern States that they háve been subjected to, what they call, "draconian" enactment made especially for them. The ULP Act applies to entire India including to the North-eastern States. The complaint of discrimination would then no longer be valid.

FOUR - The ULP Act is a comprehensive law designed to (i) ban unlawful organisations; (ii) to curb terrorist activities and the funding of terrorism; and (III) investigation, trial and punishment of persons indulging In terrorist acts, unlike the Armed Forces (Special Powers) Act which deals only with the operations of the armed forces of the Union in a disturbed area. After the, proposed amendments, ULP Act would be more comprehensive in | the sense that it would expressly permit deployment or armed forces and para-military forces of the Union, to achieve its object viz curbing terrorism. In other words, operations of the armed forces of the Union would be one of the ways of curbing terrorism. It would also mean that persons apprehended by the armed forces of the Union would be made over immediately to the nearest police

* As a number of facts, it can be said that there are two enactments for fighting militant/insurgent/terrorist organization, groups and gangs in the North-eastern States viz., the Armed Forces (Special Powers) Act whose application is limited to the North-eastern States alone and the ULP Act which extends to the whole of India including the North-eastern States.

station and would be tried in accordance with the procedure laws of the land. The prosecution too would be quicker and more effective because of the special provisions contained in Sections 44 (protection of witnesses) and 46 (admissibility of evidence collected through interception of Communications). At the same time, the accused would also get the very important safeguard contained in Section 45 of the Act which provides that no court shall take cognizance of any offience under the Act unless previous sanction therefor is granted by the appropriate government, in case the prosecuting agency proposes to proved against him for any offence in Chapter IV or Chapter VI of this Act. We may clarify that in law it lies within the discretion and judgement of the investing officer to decide, after due investigation, whether to proceed against the accused or to drop the proceedings and in case, he decides to proved against the witness, the determine the offence with which the accused in to be charged. In short, just because, a person is arrested by the armed forces acting under this Act, and is made over to thr police, the police is not bound to proceed against him only for offences under this Act, the police is free, depending upon the evidence/material gathered during investigation, to file a chargt sheet for offence under this Act or under IPC or such other appropriate enactment, as may be applicable.

7. As stated hereinabove, the ULP Act does contemplate, by necessary implication, use of armed forces or para-military forces to conduct operations and to take steps to fight and curb terrorism. It does not, however, contain any provision specifying their powers, duties and procedures relevant to their deployment. It does not also provide for an internal mechanism ensuring accountability of such forces with a view to guard against abuses and excesses by delinquent members of such forces. It is this lacuna, which

is to be supplied by, Inserting appropriate provision in the ULP Act. The provisions so introduced should be clear, unambiguous and must specify the powers of the armed forces/para military forces while acting to curb terrorist/ insurgent activities.

8. We may also refer in this connection to the necessity of creating a mechanism, which we may designate as the Grievances Cell"-- Over the years many people from the region have been complaining that among the most difficult issues is the problem faced by those who seek information about family members and friends who have been picked up and detained by armed forces or security forces. There have been a large number of cases' where those taken away without warrants have "disappeared", or ended up dead or badly injured. Suspicion and bitterness have grown as a result. There is need for a mechanism which is transparent, quick and involves authorities from concerned agencies as well as civil society groups to provide information on the whereabouts of missing persons within 24 hours.

9. To ensure public confidence in the process of detention and arrest, grievances cells are proposed to be set up in each district where armed forces are deployed; These cells will receive complaints regarding allegations of missing persons or abuse of law by security/armed forces, make prompt enquiries and furnish information to the complainant, Where, however, the complainant is not satisfied with the information furnished and is prepared to file an affidavit In support of his allegation, it shall be competent for the Cell to call upon the State level head of the concerned force or organization to enquire into the matter and report the same to the cell as early as possible, not exceeding in any event, one week. The State level officers from whom these Grievances Cells seek information

shall immediately make necessary enquiries and furnish full and correct information to the Grievances Cell as early as possible, not exceeding in any event one week. The Grievances Cells will be composed of three persons, namely, a senior member of the local administration as its chair, a Captain of the armed forces/security forces and a senior member of the local police. These will have dedicated Communications, authority to obtain Information from concerned authorities and have facilities for recording and responding to complaints. They shall locate their offices in the premises of the Sub Divisional Magistrate or in the premises of the District Magistrates, as the case may be. Such a mechanism is absolutely essential to achieve the two equally important purposes viz., (a) to infuse and instill confidence among the citizenry that the State, while deploying the armed forces of the Union to fight insurgency/ terrorism has also taken care to provide for steps to guard against abuses/excesses with a view to protect the people and to preserve their democratic and civil rights; and (b) to protect the honour and the fair name of the forces.

10. While deploying the forces under sub-section (3) the Central Government shall, by a notification published in the Gazette, specifying the State or the part of the State in which the forces would operate and the period (not exceeding six months) for which the forces shall operate. At the end of the period so specified, the Central Government shall review the situation in consultation with the State Government and check whether the deployment of forces should continue and if it is to continue for which period. This review shall take place as and when it is found necessary to continue the deployment of the forces at the expiry of the period earlier specified. It shall be permissible for the Central Government to vary the part of the State where the forces are deployed in case the earlier notification

is in respect of a part of a State. Every notification extending the period of deployment of forces or varying the area of the State, as the case may be, shall be laid on the table of both the Houses or Parliament within one month of the publication of such notification.

11. A draft, of the Bill which is recommended to be incorporated as Chapter VI A of the Unlawful Activities (Preventive) Act, 1967 is enclosed herewith. The draft bill is meant to serve as, a guide in drafting the legislation to be introduced in the Parliament. We may also mention that the Appendix to the draft incorporates the Do's and Don'ts issued by the Army and which have been approved by the Hon'ble Supreme Court of India in its decision report in Naga People's Movement for Human Rights vs. Union of India (A.I.R 1998 Supreme Court 431) as well as the additional directions given by the Hon'ble Supreme Court. However, those directions which have been already incorporated in the Bill are note repeated in the Appendix 13. A separate note submitted by Srí Sanjoy Hazarika, a Member of the Committee, is also enclosed at Annexure-XIV.

PART II

5

Federalism: Issues and Challenges

Indian federalism in its backdrop of pluralism, multiculturalism and multiple historical legacy, reinforced by historical imperatives undergoes post-colonial experiences of one kind or another, undertakes developmental agenda enunciated by the privatization, globalization- which has been perceived to be iniquitous to the South, and liberation-based armed struggles in the north and the North-east for more than half a century. Undoubtedly, Indian federalism would have to survive the critical tests of modernization and the perils of iniquitous globalization as well.

The political protests — violent or non-violent, democratic or otherwise — which do not step out of the defined parameters of the multi-national sovereignty and constitutionalism do not pose as major challenge to the Indian polity as such since the establishment of the Republic since Independence. Naturally, every democratic polity has experienced or experiences more or less similar political phenomena and changes. However, the union government possibly has not successfully addressed to situations of federal crisis in the north and the North-East. On occasions, the issues about the juxtaposition of human security vis-a-vis national security have been raised within a rational political discourse.

Periodically, the union government might have attempted at giving a durable political solution to the issues arising out of armed national liberation movements- which the Indian media indiscriminately and a little bit unfairly labels as terrorism *per se.* The international law discourse is a bit different though. Experts and statesmen are in search of alternative and viable solutions in lieu of further advancing half a century old counterproductive repressive and coercive measures.

Notwithstanding the political spaces for secession and external self-determination, and customary or general international law provisions and apart from the ordinary constituent states, post-independence Indian constitutionalism has created positive spaces for extraordinary states in order to meet the multiple historical contingencies.

Associate[d] state- the 35th Constitutional amendment state has been a ‘ unique historical category. The 35th amendment associate state of Sikkim [see Constitution article 2A and 10th schedule in 1975] has exercised all authority in all sense of the term barring, defence, external affairs, Communications and social welfare. The next category of special state is article 370 state of Jammu and Kashmir which had adopted its own separate constitution on 17 November, 1956. These two constitutional states *sui generis* have been recognized by the Constitution, let alone the misgivings of the union government.

Some of the ongoing ethnic rebellions or, small tribal armed struggles confined within the existing states did not conjecture, in their propositions, meta-constitutional arrangements whatever. Their outer limits are article 244 [a} statehood, and even characterized by Darjeeling Hill council model. We address to the challenges and issues of the day. Dialogues do also figure in one or two federal political space, and the outcome are awaited; judicious assessments could follow the tangible outcomes once they are made public.

Indian Federal Question

Indian federal question has been in the public domain for a long time — starting from the Government of India Act, 1935, Cabinet Mission recommendation to set up Indian confederation to Quit India AICC resolution, 1942, and Nehru's Objective resolution, 22nd January, 1947 placed before the Constituent Assembly, which recommended that residuary powers of the federation be left with the constituent units. The partition fever had persisted long after the partition and pre-empted the materialization of the envisaged federation. Analysts of all ideological pursuasions characterise Indian federation as quasi or, cooperative or, in whatever they desire to perceive of, by overlooking the building block- parameters of making India.

The evasion of the federal question resulted to DMK's secessionist proposal in the 1960s, rise of regional and subnational issues in the 1960s, formation of regional coalition governments in the states, Administrative Reforms Commission, Akali Dal resolutions, West Bengal document 1977 on federation, insurgencies of all kinds and subsequently thereafter, the constitution of Sarkaria Commission for restructuring the center-state relations in a tangible way. Sarkaria Commission recommendations, 1988 had suggested modest reforms only, whereas the regional parties in the country had strongly urged for reconstituting a federation, after making necessary constitutional amendments. [see several dozen of memoranda submitted by regional parties-vol. II, Report]

In response to Sarkaria Commission recommendations, Government of Assam-High Power Committee on the

Recommendations of the Sarkaria Commission on Centre-state relations,1988 observed, among others, "1.2. It is necessary to review all the existing entries in the Union, State and Concurrent Lists. A review should also be made about the residual power of legislation vested in Article 248."[p.3. para1.2]. It also observed, "Before the Parliament imposes any limitation on taxes on mineral rights, there should be mandatory and effective consultation with the State Government" [p.19. para 13.5.12].

The regional party in power at that time in 1986 at Mangaldoi general body conference has urged upon the union government to concede -*'atmaniyantron'{ sic. qualified]* to the people and state of Assam- the resolution stands as such till date. The ruling regional party in Assam had stood for federation or, probably even more, as the record may be put straight.

Report of the National Commission to Review the Working of the Constitution, March 31, 2002 had not dwelt upon federal questions even peripherally, as the terms of reference issued on 22 February, 2000 had been incredibly narrow. It has, however, noted the existence of a watered down federalism. [p. 27, Report ,ULPC, 2002]. p.3 federalism

Federal Question & NES

The NE states bear peculiar and singular political characteristics in terms of its spacial relationship with the Indian Union — a creation of Indian Independence Act, 1947, and concomitant merger or annexation of princely states. Some states had disputed the merger/annexation process by way of insurgency, belligerency and extremist militant armed struggles. It may be recalled that had the Plan Balkan materialized in 1947, at least a dozen nation states should have emanated in the Indian subcontinent. In the nine-year long dialogue, an outfit of Nagaland

[Nagalim] has been negotiating for a separate Constitution of Nagaland with the union government. In the proposed federal arrangement, government of India could retain four powers exclusively or, jointly with Nagaland. The matter cannot be elaborated upon further as the ongoing Indo-Naga talk continues and progresses.

Assam had been annexed to a foreign state in 1826 following an agreement reached between two foreign powers in total exclusion of sovereign Asom state. The dual trajectory of Assamese nationalism shared a single curve till 1979. Gopinath Bardoloi's persistent demand for a separate Constitution of Assam in 1946, language movement in 1960s [sic. Cf. linguistic European nation state], anti-alien movement since 1979, refinery and other autonomy movements characterize the common curve. The regional party's demand for Right to Self-determination [possibly within Indian federation] in 1986, organized youths and students' demand for greater autonomy comparable to that of J&K are political expressions of Asom national question. This is trajectory I of Asom national question.

Trajectory II is symbolised by ULFA's demand for sovereignty. As the pre-dialogue preparation has just started, we hold our subjective opinion on this sensitive subject. Public opinion might have been divided- only a statewide opinion poll would be able to give certain clear indications; rest are subjective conjectures of dreamy intellectuals and heaven for paparazzis or, embedded journalism.

National Liberation movements occurred in the last half a century in acquired territories like Manipur and Tripura and also in Nagaland [Naga hills at a point of time-excluded areas], which consider themselves as NSGT in international law parlance. Things had settled in Mizoram; however, some traces are visible even today.

The rest of the NE states also experience armed struggles — both ethnic and national. The armed struggles occur, and the AFSPA, 1958 is yet to be repealed. Justice Jeevan Reddy Report, 2005 has recommended repeal of the AFSPA, and also inclusion of certain ambiguous provisions in the UPA, 1967 as amended in 2002. The AFSPA has supposedly sprouted multiple insurgencies due to entrenched fear psychosis of the imposed terror.

Questions remain in the public domain about the National Liberation Movements, autonomy demands, national and sub-national questions, federalization of the polity, amendments of the Constitution, and restructuring the existing overcentralized constitutional arrangements-whatever.

The union government has no alternative than finding out a complete, and durable equitable federal solution to the ongoing federal crisis. Piecemeal or cosmetic approaches had outlived: their contingent purposes and expediency. It is conceivable that military solution and repressive measures, as envisaged long back has been found be counter-productive in the long run. There probably had never been a crisis that could not be resolved given a strong political resolve and commitment.

FURTHER READING

1. Report of the Sarkaria Commission, part II- Memoranda of the regional parties on devolution of powers to the states;
2. Report of the National Commission to Review the Working of the Constitution, 2002;
3 AIRPF, Symphony of Freedom—Papers on Nationality Question, Hyderbad, 1996;
4. Naorem Sanajaoba:
   [a] Basic Issues on Centre-State Relations, ed., 1985, Omsons, ND;

[b] *Law and Society*, 2001, Mittal Publications, ND, 'Rise and Fall of Federations', pp 206-250;

[c] *Human Rights*, ed, 1994, Omsons, ND, 'Right of Nations to Self-Determination', pp. 38-65;

[d] *Right of Oppressed Nations* [And Peoples], 1985, Omsons, ND; 'The Legitimacy of State Autonomy', pp. 31-66;

[e] *Human Rights in the New Millennium*, 2000, Manas, ND; 'New Constitution', pp. 14-35;

[f] *Human Rights Current Issues,* 2004, Omsons, ND; 'Constitution Review Commission', pp. 102-120

[g] *Manipur Puwaari-Kunmathoishuba Chahicha,* 2006, National Research Centre, Imphal, pp 1- 346; see his writings since 1966-2007.

5. Publications from the North-Eastern region since 1947-2007 including the booklets distributed by the insurgent organizations or their websites.

6

Ethnic Conflicts and Resolutions

ETHNIC THOUGHT

The ethnic thought and engagement is one of the *most fundamental issues of the contemporary world,* which in its new order provides for political devolution on the one hand and economic integration on the other hand. Fundamentalisation of faith and values have replaced the ideological battle between capitalism and socialism by shifting the goal posts of the nations, ethnoses and states.

Ethnic phenomena, existentialism range from ethnicity to ethnocentrism and even to the brink of ethnocide or, ethnic cleansing of the Bosnia kind. It also spreads over the phenomena of ethnic mobilization, ethnic nationalism and self-determination- internal or, external or, both. The genesis lies in identity- consciousness, exclusiveness, perceived insecurity and imagined threats from *others. 'The US and THEM'* cognition is the very basis of ethnicity and its manifold phenomena.

The phenomena have been characterized by violent conflicts, xenophobia, chauvinism of varying degrees, virulent forms of ethnic nationalism elsewhere, fragmentation of the colonial glues that, among others, rendered new ethnic constructions or even tribal conglomerates in the NE region of India into a cauldron. For historical and geo-strategic reasons, the North-Eastern States of India is unique in more than one sense. Ethnic groups, indigenous nations and three major nation-states of Assam, Manipur and Tripura of the past two millennia give testimony to the emergence of new. Primodialists who have parted with the basic tenets of old primodialists like language, religion and culture following the adoption of Christianity, English or corrupted Assamese dialect and western cultural models. Ethnicity in the primordial sense lost the essence save the attachment to land, and natural resources. The new ethnicity switches over to instrumentalism or, transactionalism. The Meeteis by and large have also proselytized to Hinduism not so long ago, and de-culturalised themselves by parting with their primordial concerns. Ethnicity is no more the same and the same is the ethnic philosophy. Insurgency, national liberation movements, political bargaining violent conflicts and some events of ethnic cleansing bear testimony to the NES specifics. The general pattern also is tangible in the phenomena. Issues of internal colonialism, need for self-governance and sub-ethnic territoriality are equally significant.

CONTEXTUALIZATION

General

Political systems like Totalitarianism, Liberal democracy and Socialist or peoples' democracy present contextual responses to ethnic phenomena in varying degrees. Ethnicity survives in the contexts.

Silencing or subjugation of ethnic phenomena could be done in Totalitarian, fundamentalist, authoritarian systems for a period of time. National socialism of the Third Reich made futile attempts at a heavy cost of millions of human lives; the ideology dies down and the Jews survive even today. Small scale Talibanisation, political Islam, political Hinduism or political Christianity find their ready-made and predictable answers in similar vein. The price humanity has to pay is a little high though.

Liberal democracy could assiduously afford to ethno-nationalism, sovereign linguistic nation states in Europe, pan-African tribalism, poly-ethnic political arrangements, short-lived secessionist ambitions of the affluent ethnic groups in Europe, UK and Indian republic as well as the impoverished sub-nationalities or ethnoses in the country. Ethnicity does not leave the liberal democratic agenda.

Socialist states like the Peoples Republic of China, launch state action against Han chauvinists consistently, set up standing commissions to take care of the smallest ethnic groups in a plethora of 55- minority polity, share political and economic power with the 55 ethnic groups, programme pro-nationalities education in the state universities, and create autonomous region or areas. The Han chauvinists have to be re-educated in the civil society or the prison house if necessary.

The former Soviet Union also made elaborate constitutional arrangements even upto the extent of granting Right to secede to constituent states (*read* republics). Ethnic uprisings could be ruled out, yet ethnicity remains. The party and socialist governance had not only to eliminate last traces and obnoxious public memories of the czar, feudal remnants and relics on the one hand, but also to reeducate or prevent and hit back on the arrogant Chinese warlords and Han chauvinists who did not practice national equality. The Cultural revolution had earned mixed responses.

Ethnic cleansing witnessed in the West like the Balkans, in Africa like Burundi and Rwanda or, even in the microscopic tiny hills of early state of Manipur in the 1990s or, ethnocentricity of the English or Enoch Powel disciples or the KKK of the USA could not be even thought of in socialist ethnic thought. The economic equality, national equality or equality at birth of individual human beings find little access to dominant ethnoses or leaders in some areas, whereas the socialist thought had taken care of the reactionaries in the regime.

NES Specific

The NES has its own unique historical experiences, legacy, primordialism, polyethnic consciousness, ethnic mobilization, small sub-nationalities syndrome within and without. A definition could be evasive- the issue remains in a number of perceptions- apparent, real or, imagined or even critically engineered to make geo-strategic considerations of super power compatible with the instrumentalist agenda. In bad cases, ethnicity explodes loud.

General

Ethnic groups — big or small — contest over ancestral lands, territoriality, resources, power structure- traditional authority vis-a-vis the modern industry-driven bureaucratic state and above, all the domain of political or cultural consciousness. Marginalisation of ethnic groups and subsequent ethnic mobilization are common elsewhere. The ethnic existential phenomena are transformed to social conflicts, pressure group action and violent conflicts. In some cases, legitimate ethnic nationalists claim the peoples' right to self-determination. Enclaves and tiny ethnic groups are not favourably placed in the exercise of the right to self-determination. The post world war II de-colonisation process render the principle obvious.

NES Specific

The North-eastern states is a cultural-geographic embodiment of three early states of Assam, Manipur and Tripura with at least fifty ethnic groups, and four created states with another fifty ethnic groups. Ethnic contests over domain and space are quite natural. Legitimate peoples (nations) in the NES are claiming their right of the people to self-determination by resorting to military means. Ethnic cleansing, intra-ethnic conflicts occurred along with the contest over territoriality. Vain attempts to balkanize early states have been made thereby sharpening the intra-ethnic tensions. However, the established **'Uti Possidetis Juris'** norm applies invariably. Certain re-processed polyethnic subnationalities make claims in terms of misrepresented irredentism; it, however, does not hold water and lacks irrefutable evidence.

General

Totalitarianism and authoritarianism has the inbuilt ethnic subjugation philosophy, ideology and structural-violence structure as found in the Taliban faith, fundamentalist Islamic or Hindu tenets or, political Christianity as seen in Ulster or Europe. Egalitarian philosophy based on intra- ethnic harmony has case with totalitarianism, fundamentalism and authoritarianism. Enhanced, sharpened ethnocentrism could also lead to the evils of fundamentalism.

Liberal democracy is contending with dominance, hegemonic control, partition, ethnic cleansing and other forms of conflicts. Ethnocentric parties occasionally occupy the central space in several western states and even in India that witnessed Sikh massacre in 1984, Muslim massacre in Gujarat and the cataclysmic 1947 partition massacre to the tune of millions. Ideological battle and debate continues. Liberal democracy has also devised cantonisation, federalism, even confederalism to tackle the issue. **Consociational** arrangements make room for proportional representation in the state structure, veto power of the minority on vital issues of the national minority and egalitarian power-sharing.

Peoples democracy or, socialist system has wiped out the adverse fall-out of ethnicity and promoted ethnic harmony by making heavy assault on incorrigible chauvinist elements, war lords, obnoxious feudal elements of all hues and pretensions. The party and mass line weeds out the anti-social elements, groups while following the principle of socialist governance.

NES Specific

Paradox I-- Conjecturing the creation of one hundred independent or, constituent ethnic states for one hundred tribes appears to be untenable. The right of the people to self-determination has to be exercised reasonably by contextualizing viability, common historical experiences and advancing the intra-ethnic solidarity.

Paradox II--Fragmentation of early states is not an attempt towards achieving ethnic harmony, but perpetuating Lebanonisation and ethnic cleansing of all persuasions. The binding rule is the international law principle of Uti Possidetis Juris.

Paradox III--Ethnicity can not be rationalized and made a subject of fruitful discourse in the process of governance and constitutional re-arrangements whatsoever. Ethnicity is one of the most fundamental principles of contemporary world which has to be addressed.

RATIONAL DISCOURSE

Ethnicity, nation, nation-state, post-nation and conflict-situations are subject of rigorous academic exercise in the universities, institutes. The world orders — successive, old and new or envisaged — have to address the issue by active engagements. Rational discourse make inroads in theoretical constructs, possibilities, statecrafts — real or idealpolitik and the debate is alive.

Some of the perspectives are:

> Firstly, in the long run, ethnicity would be returned to shades by the transcending states and economic orders, based on egalitarianism, overarching EQUALITY AND JUSTICE principle. Secondly, the ongoing ethnogenesis process could lead to the end of polyethnicism at a point of time and, fusion or assimilation could take place. English people is a fusion of the Angles, Jutes and Saxons, whereas the fusion stops at the ethnic traffic point where the Scotch, the Welsh, the Irish and the English, as well as the polyethnic Asian, non-British migrants meet each other. Could there be another fusion is a question mark. Thirdly, arbitration, negotiation, consociational arrangements and federalism compounded by multiculturalism or pluralism could rationalize ethnic contests.
>
> The ethnicity, polyethnicity and ethnic conflicts in the NES bear some of the salient features of general, if not a heavy universal ethnic laws, as no such law has ever existed. Certain characteristics like unique historical experiences, early states, existence of a galaxy of ethnic groups whatsoever, ongoing liberation movements and ethnological phenomena bear the stamp of NES specifics.

7

Structure of Negotiation Between Metropolitan Power & National Liberation Authority (21 C. NSGT Issues)

After the passing of the Indian Independence Act, 1947,[1] lapse of British paramountcy in native states and colonial rule, in British Indian provinces, consequent upon merger of states to the Indian Dominion on the one hand, insufficient attention given to indigenous national questions in the North-Eastern region,[2] armed national liberation movements occur in Manipur[3] and the region for more than half a century.[4] As Joshua S. Goldstein observes 'Substate and Supranational actors influence 21st century world politics. In the N.E, region, it is equally true.'

Civil society remains restive, human rights violated routinely and paradigm for durable peace and development, found missing. Union Government blames peripheral secessionism, and the national liberation movement authority denounces colonial rule and foreign military occupation.[5] These are the two versions, advanced by the two belligerent parties. Some fanatical sections believe in military repression of the political issue but it is a foolish adventurism of wild war-mongers.

The 20th century has evolved certain benchmarks which would pave way for solutions of issues. Conflict resolution is a multipronged approach. One of the rational approaches found suitable in such a situation of protracted hostility is the search for negotiation-paradigm, some of which have been successfully ušed by parties in advancing their respective bargaining positions. Human security, International laws and standard state practices remain the benchmark.

A couple of workable paradigms in the similar situations are analysed. Other approaches are also not ruled out. The paper takes up rather inclusive approach, and does not rule out better and just options *sui generis* or otherwise.

Case Studies

From South East Asia — Vietnam; Middle- East-Palestine; Europe-Northern Ireland; Asia-Pacific-East Timor; and South Asia- Sri-Lanka (Tamil Eelam).

Vietnam

Before de-colonization started in the 1900s all over the world, Dullesian doctrine of Domino effect in Indo-china, rise of Cold war and third Communist International made dent on the geo-strategic significance of Vietnam and Indo-china to the Western vital interest. Vietnamese liberation forces, insignificant in comparison to French colonial forces in 1950s and American imperialist forces in 1950s onwards, had humbled both the colonial powers one after another.[6]

French forces surrendered in 1954, and USA's more than half a million soldiers, air and naval forces supported by the largest ever presence of the CIA covert invasion surrendered to the North Vietnamese national liberation forces on 30th April, 1975 after killing 2 million vietnamese and ruining the soil for another millennium due to massive bombing of all kind for decades.

Three broad kind of negotiations or International conferences had been conducted. In order to restore peace and development in partitioned Vietnam viz., I-Terminal talks following decisive military defeat of the occupation and colonial forces of the West; II-Constructive negotiations that paved way for shaping the end-result of the hostilities and, III- Secret negotiation

Pattern I

- 1954 July Conference in Geneva that made North Vietnam independent, and ensured elections in South Vietnam (divided at the 17th parallel by the west). USA formed SEATO (c. 1975) Guarantors: China, France, UK and USSR
- 27 January 1973 Paris Accord: USA, 2 Vietnams, Vietcong met at Paris [8] that ensured International supervision of the cease-fire, ensured American retreat from occupied country. [Details, see annexed document in the chapter]

Pattern II

- Geneva Summit of 1955 to ease Cold War.
- 1967 Johnson-Kosygin talks to end Vietnam War;
- May 1968 talks between US and North Vietnam.

Pattern III

Secret negotiations in 1970, July 1971 and 1973, Kissinger and North Vietnamese leadership in Paris. Since 1970, Henry Kissinger networked for talks with North Vietnam.[9] The secret talks made the official negotiations successful.

After tackling Vietnam, Vietnamese expert Kissinger wrote [9a] the DICTUM — "the guerrilla army wins 25 long 25 it can keep from losing;-the conventional army is bound to lose unless it wins decisively" (diplomacy p. 629). Talk has been calibrated on pattern II constructive talks and pattern III secret talks, facilitated the end of hostilities on the one hand, and resulted to culmination of the conflicts at diplomatic, political and military levels.

Palestine

Barring USA and Israel, literally the entire world stood behind the formation of Palestine state and terminating Arab-Israel conflict.[10] The UN general assembly, security council and all the machineries have recurrently justified Palestinians rights to self-determination. In 2004 and also 2005, the USA prepares a road map for the emerging Palestine state in the near future.

Pre-1990 agreements include: 1949 Armistice agreement between Arab states and Israel, 1975 Egypt" and Israel Troops Disengagement Agreement, and 1978 Camp David agreement which denied RSD of the Palestinians (negated security council resolution No. 242 and 338), yet provided a framework for peace in the Middle East, to be followed by the 1979 Peace Treaty.

International conferences, *International guarantors are the sine qua non of scripting and building-up peace* in the Middle east; the conflict resolution had never been left to the choice of the warring parties. The most complicated and time-consuming peace building process demonstrates the fundamentals of peace negotiations. The following international conferences and agreements accumulated to the present uncompleted peace-building process.[11] They are:

1990s

- October 1991 Madrid International Conference (USA forced Likud leadership of Israel to conf.)
- 1992 Simon peres-PLO secret talks in Norway.
- 1993 September, Oslo accord (l), No longer all Arab issue, but identified as bilateral issue.
- 1993 Yatshak Rabin- Arafat signed DOP (Declaration of Principles) in Washington,
- 1994 Cairo Agreement,
- Autonomy for Gaza.
- 1995 September Oslo (II) Accord- Peace process continues; [See document appended]
- 28 September, 1995 Taba Agreement: way to election to Palestinian Legislative Council.
- January 5, 1997 Hebron Agreement: for withdrawal of Israeli troops from Hebron.

Wye I (October 1998): To implement Oslo l- to root Hamas terrorists.

Wye II (5 September 1999). Follow up to Oslo, 11% of West Bank Lands to Palestinians, 40% of territory occupied in 1967 to Palestinians and Palestinians not to make unilateral declaration of Independence.

2000s

Wye II (phase III, January 2000): Framework agreement: Sharm El Sheikh Agreement (1990): On permanent state of Israel and Palestine Authority. Geneva (unofficial accord, 2003 end).

US provides road map for Palestine state (2005) in near future.[12] Sharm al- Sheikh (Sharon-Abbas) Summit,

February, 2005: No specific goal international community, interspersed by wars, hostilities, assassinations, Intifada ultimately aim at restoring peace in the middle-east.

The entire process had been for half a century, supported by the United Nations by resolutions that endorse legitimate right to self-determination of Palestinians. Talks are found protracted and long. The USA as superpower takes initiative to install a democratic Palestine state in 2005, after Arafat's demise. Wars, intifada and Summits happen intermittently thereby shaping the goal. Negotiations are indispensable at one stage or another even in situations of deep conflicts.

Northern Ireland

No other Intra-European conflict resolution and political negotiation could ever have been better and smoother than the peace process that culminated to 10 April, 1998 Good Friday Agreement,[13] signed by the British government and IRA leadership, fully guaranteed by no less than American President Mr. Bill Clinton and senate leader of the USA- Mr. George Mitchell, who presided over the 22 month-long nonstop negotiation. Negotiation does not have any break.

The 'international guarantor' is the most indispensable cornerstone of a meaningful negotiation between metropolitan power and a rebel group like IRA. Former colonial countries, which look towards British paradigm and model have to take the said agreement seriously. The guarantor has a role to prevent the talk from sliding down and generates a possible result. It is not luxury.

The precondition for such a negotiation is that it has been preceded by a 'Framework' declaration like the December 15, 1994 Downing Street declaration'[14] made by prime minister John Major.

John Major lacked the minimum 2/3 Majority in the British parliament to clinch a deal like the 10 April 1998 Good Friday agreement and so, his party did not outside a declaration. The government party should have compatibility with necessary parliamentary strength.

Only the Labour Party, which had 2/3 majority in the house had the compatibility to make a major deal like the 1998 agreement. These are the parameters for hammering out a successful (read-not bogus and fake) negotiation in similar situation elsewhere in the world.

The background of US senate leader George Mitchell is that he is a Catholic (similar to the IRA, not the British Protestant majority in UK), born of an Arab mother. His bio-data carries credibility for adequate neutrality besides his being the senate leader of the USA senate- the upper house.

The negotiating team includes support of US President, two prime ministers, US senate leader (President) and eight political parties, which referred the agreement to their respective general councils/ bodies (Plenum) and put the same to referendum. In spite of these basic negotiating mechanisms, certain hiccups had been reported later on. Downing Street declaration, 1994 had officially recognised 'self-determination right of Northern Ireland that led to negotiation. [See document appended]

Timor-Liste (Former East Timor)

Tomor-Liste was in the list of NSGT (non-self-governing territory) of Committee of 24, till it became independent on 20 May, 2002, following a UN organised referendum.[15] The conventional political negotiations, guarantor operating behind the negotiation were not found, because of the UN intervention through the General Assembly and the Security council, which declared Indonesian invasion, occupation of East Timor immediately after Portugal left the small country illegal, unjustified by all standards, customary international law, provisions of the right to self-determination (*jus cogens*).

Government of Indonesia a close strategically of the USA[16] which had a hand in Indonesian annexation of East Timor for serving American strategic interest (not law) advanced three plausible arguments in defence of annexation and rule of ET: l) ET had historical and cultural ties with Indonesia in the past; II) Indonesia had annexed ET due to invitation by 4 political parties and resolution of ET Peoples Consultative Committee (popular choice misrepresented) and III) ET will not be economically viable. In the UN and outside, colleagues on ET continued. The dialogues shape the political status of ET.

UN General Assembly recommended consultation with all political parties, rejected Indonesia's perfidy under international law, and rendered UN intervention in ET, Chapter XI and XII of the UN Charter, originally meant for Trusteeship only have been extended by recognising 'After-Acquired NSGT' of ET International conferencing etc. had been conducted under UN aegis.[17]

The frente revolutionariea de Timor teste independente (FRETLIN) and its military wing Forces armada de Libetacao National de Timor Leste (FALINTIL) fought out Indonesian occupation army from the very time of Indonesian annexation, that rendered the resistance spontaneous and credible to the international community.

The UNAMET (United Nations Mission in ET), UNTAET (United Nations Transitional Administration in ET), UN-Multinational Force for ET to protéct UNAMET since 1999, UNMISET (United Nations Mission for Support in ET) after 2002 have operated in the de-colonisation of ET. International community and opinion had the space within these UN machineries.[18]

Tamil Eelam

Norwegian government has acted as facilitator in the negotiation between Sri Lanka Government and the LTTE leadership. Until N. Ireland case, they do not have international guarantors and do not acquire sufficient ground in the talks. The process could resume in the near future.

In 1985, multilateral talks, Thimpu principles have been identified. The 1987 Indo-Sri Lanka Agreement led to disaster, IPKF intervention without explicit acceptance of LTTE, massacre of Tamils and tragic assassination of Indian Prime Minister who made out the 1987 agreement and IPKF fiasco. LTTE's active acquiescence was missing and that led to the collapse of the agreement.

2003 LTTE blueprint[19] demands Immediate execution of Tamil Eelam by the occupation. Sri Lankan army, respect for 3 Thimpu principles (self-determination), reaching a final settlement in a frame (cl. 9), reference to the International Court of Justice in case of 3-member tribunal's inability to resolve disagreement (cl. 22), among others.

Shri Lanka government considers the blueprint for negotiation as de facto declaration of Tamil Eelam. The negotiation could be resumed in the near future with the same facilitator i.e. Norway.

The North-East Region

The select tested structures of negotiation do not close options and possibilities in the conduct of international relations. Insurgency in the NE region is one of the oldest in the world.[20]

The 'effective' national liberation organisations, which have been so listed by GOI as unlawful organisations and GOI may study model for negotiations. A faction of NSCN of Nagaland continues dialogue on Sovereignty of Nagaland with GOI since 1997 for less than a decade. The progress is not made public, and process lacks transparency, interlocutor who is domestic and not bipartisan,[21] belonging to one of the parties in the conflict is not neutral.

The GOl-NSCN-faction negotiation lacks the essential transparency, and other essential criteria of standard negotiations.

NOTES & REFERENCES

1. Annexation of Manipur, 1949, PDM, Manipur p, 7-46.
2. Naorem Sanajaoba, *Human Rights—Current Issues*, Omsons, New Delhi; State repression and Nations questions in North-East; pp. 166-100, as regards NLM, study UN materials-c. 24, 4th committee of GA, S.C etc..
3. Id. p. 142-162;
4. *Ibid.*
5. Id. p. 144,-Blue-hills colonialism; see N. Sanajaoba, *Manipur Puwari*, 1997. 23-35; 146-164; cf. N. Sanajaoba, *Manipur Puwari Kunmathoisuba Chahicha*, 2005 (up), NRC for elaborate details and cornprehensive study;
6. Henry Kissinger, *Diplomacy*, Simon & Schuster, London, 1995, Vietnam, pp. 620-702;
7. Id. p. 661-665; 683-687; 693-697; In 1954, Geneva Accords, nine countries 6 declarations & 3 agreements;
8. Id. p. 635, Soviet Union lacked interest;
9. Id. p. 665, *Peace Negotiations*, pp 678-679, 697-698;

9a. Id. p. 629, *On Vietnam*, See Pater Calvocoressi., *World Politics 1945-2000*, Pearson, 2001 pp. 528-946; Jasliua *S.* Goldstein, *International Relations*, Pearson, 2003, pp. 42,80.

10. *op. cit.*, Peter Calvocoressi. pp. 380-445;
11. The Palestine Problem; Aggression, Resistance. ...... USSR

Academy of Sciences, Moscow, 1984, pp. 105-139; 8-39; see *Journal of Palestine Studies* (JPS),

On State formation:

JPS XXI No. 1, 1990; XXIV No. 4, (Yezld Sayigh, sovereignty.....of Palestine state, pp. 5-19) 1995;

On Accords:

XXXIII No. l, 2003; XXX No. 2, 2001 (Camp David), XXI No. 2. 1992 9 Madrid conference); XXV No 4. 1996 (Oslo Accord); XXX No. 2, 2001 (Jerusalem) Note; Feb 2005, Sharon-abbas Summit does not dwell upon east Jerusalem, cf demand of PLO; XXX No. 2, 2001 (Oslo Agreement); XXXII No. 2. 2003 Oslo), XXIII No. 2, 1994 (UN-Resolution 242); XXXIII No. l. 2003 (Camp David); XXIII No. 4, 1994 (Israel-PLO Agreement); XXIII No 3, 1994 (Oslo Accord) etc.

12. Palestine state inevitable *op. cit.,* Peter Calvocoressi, p. 445, see Civil Society Peace initiative—the Geneva Accord, 10 October, 2004 in JPS XXXIII No. 2, Winter 2004, pp. 81-101. Art. 4 provides for international border of Palestine and Israel as on 4 June 1969.
13. N. Sanajaoba, *Belfast Agreement*, 1998 in Eikhoigee Yaaol, April, 1999 pp-3-4 and 16;
14. British attitude to RSD, Framework agreement, Downing Street Declaration, 1993, see N. Sanajnoba, *Right of Oppressed Nations (And Peoples),* Omson, ND, 1990 p. 102-103,82; see Karl Marx, Irish Question.
15. Oppeheim's International Law, vol l, 2003, p.196; Ingrid Deller, *The Law of War*, Cambridge, 2003, pp. 194, 344 ((, cf. Special Colloquium on EAST TIMOR, 4 July, 1999, IPSA, Main Colloquist N. Sanajaoba. Brief comment on some dissimilarities between Manipur and ET by O. Bhogen (Thrust on Christianity factor). See Sanajaoba, East Timorgee Ningtamba, Poknapham 5 June, 2002 (celebration 20 May 2002 by Manipur Solidarity on ET) and also his speeeh on UN day, 24 October, 1999 in Poknapham Oct. 23, 2000 plus other views, in *Sangai Express*, 31 Oct. 1999- 'In step with the United Nations'.
16. James Dunn, International Law and the Question of East Timor, 1994, pp. 81-101. 65-103 (UN Adms, and de-colonisation)
17. See UN, General Assembly, June, 1999, Special Committee (i.e. c 24) on East Timor for details.

18. On Post-annexation internationalisation of East Timor and UN intervention in right time, see *op. cit.* Joshua S. Goldstein, pp 191, 275; Peter Calvocorssi, p. 561; *Op. cit,* James Crawford pp. 309, 304,435, see NSGT, pp. 92-98, 358-363.
19. LTTE blue print cites; "consistent with the principles of the rule of law, the human rights and equality of all persons and the right to self-determination of popples," *The Hindu* full Text 2 November 2003, p. 10; *Frontline* S. 12. 2003 pp. 4-15, LTTE proposals for negotiation.

    cf. N Sanajaoba, *op. cit.* pp. 83,100 on Tamil Eelam and also his book, *Law & Society* 2010 on Tamils, 177-205;
20. *op. cit.,* N. Sanajaoba, Human Rights Current Issues, 'India's Restive Region; pp-142-165; and NQs pp. 166-180;
21. Joint communique Dt. 11 July, 2002 Amsterdam provides in para 2 as: "The Government of India recognised the unique history and situation of Nagas. . . ."

    After 8 years of talks in March, 2005 GOI and the faction start taking up substantive Issues, *Telegraph*, Guwahati 10 March, 2005; IRA-GB non-stop negotiation in 1998 took pretty long 22 months, USA remaining the guarantor.
22. Law Department, G.U. Assam, A REPORT Open Forum, GOI-ULTRA Negotiation, 22 January, 2005.

    In May, 2005, ULFA in Assam signals its possible negotiation with GOI exclusively on Assam's sovereignty. UNLF in November, 2004 has proposed referendum of people of Manipur on sovereignty and independence. PLA (of RPF) states that it will not de-commission weapons till a final political settlement could be reached on the independence of Manipur. There is little headway in 2007.

Document

Agreement Between the Government of the United Kingdom of Great Britain and Northern Ireland and the Government of Ireland

The British and Irish Governments

Welcoming the strong commitment to the Agreement reached on 10th April 1998 by themselves and other participants in the multi-party talks and set out in Annex 1 to this Agreement (hereinafter "the Multi-Party Agreement");

Considering that the Multi-Party Agreement offers an opportunity for a new beginning in relationships within Northern Ireland, within the island of Ireland and between the peoples of these islands;

Wishing to develop still further the unique relationship between their peoples and the close cooperation between their countries as friendly neighbours and as partners in the European Union;

Reaffirming their total commitment to the principles of democracy and non-violence which have been fundamental to the multi-party talks;

Reaffirming their commitment to the principles of partnership, equality and mutual respect and to the protection of civil, political, social, economic and cultural rights in their respective jurisdictions;

Have agreed as follows:

Article 1

The Two Governments

(i) recognise the legitimacy of whatever choice is freely

exercised by a majority of the people of Northern Ireland with regard to its status, whether they prefer to continue to support the Union with Great Britain or a sovereign united Ireland;

(ii) recognise that it is for the people of the island of Ireland alone, by agreement between the two parts respectively and without external impediment, to exercise their right of self-determination on the basis of consent, freely and concurrently given, North and South, to bring about a united Ireland, if that is their wish, accepting that this right must be achieved and exercised with and subject to the agreement and consent of a majority of the people of Northern Ireland;

(iii) acknowledge that while a substantial section of the people in Northern Ireland share the legitimate wish of a majority of the people of the island of Ireland for a united Ireland, the present wish of a majority of the people of Northern Ireland, freely exercised and legitimate, is to maintain the Union and accordingly, that Northern Ireland's status as part of the United Kingdom reflects and relies upon that wish; and that it would be wrong to make any change in the status of Northern Ireland save with the consent of a majority of its people;

(iv) affirm that, if in the future, the people of the island of Ireland exercise their right of self-determination on the basis set out *in* sections (i) and (ii) above to bring about a united Ireland, it will be a binding obligation on both Governments to introduce and support in their respective Parliaments legislation to give effect to that wish;

(v) affirm that whatever choice is freely exercised by a majority of the people of Northern Ireland, the power of the sovereign government with jurisdiction there shall be exercised with rigorous impartiality on behalf of all the people in the diversity of their identities and traditions and shall be founded on the principles of full respect for, and equality of, civil, political, social and cultural rights, of freedom from discrimination for all citizens, and of parity of esteem and of just and equal treatment for the identity, ethos and aspirations of both communities;

(vi) recognise the birthright of all the people of Northern Ireland to identify themselves and be accepted as Irish or British, or both, as they may so choose, and accordingly confirm that their right to hold both British and Irish citizenship is accepted by both Governments and would not be affected by any future change in the status of Northern Ireland.

Article 2

The two Governments affirm their solemn commitment to support, and where appropriate implement, the provisions of the Multi-Party Agreement. In particular there shall be established in accordance with the provisions of the Multi-Party Agreement immediately on the entry into force of this Agreement, the following institutions:

(i) a North/South Ministerial Council;

(ii) the implementation bodies referred to in paragraph 9 (ii) of the section entitled "Strand Two" of the Multi-Party Agreement;

(iii) a British-Irish Council;

(iv) a British-Irish Intergovernmental Conference.

Article 3

1. This Agreement shall replace the Agreement between the British and Irish Governments done at Hillsborough on 15th November 1985 which shall cease to have effect on entry into force of this Agreement.
2. The Intergovernmental Conference established by Article 2 of the aforementioned Agreement done on 15th November 1985 shall cease to exist on entry into force of this Agreement.

Article 4

1. It shall be a requirement for entry into force of this Agreement that:
   (a) British legislation shall have been enacted for the purpose of implementing the provisions of Annex A to the section entitled "Constitutional Issues" of the Multi-Party Agreement;
   (b) the amendments to the Constitution of Ireland set out in Annex B to the section entitled "Constitutional Issues" of the Multi-Party Agreement shall have been approved by Referendum;
   (c) such legislation shall have been enacted as may be required to establish the institutions referred to in Article 2 of this Agreement.
2. Each Government shall notify the other in writing of the completion, so far as it is concerned, of the requirements for entry into force of this Agreement. This Agreement shall enter into force on the date of the receipt of the later of the two notifications.
3. Immediately on entry into force of this Agreement,

the Irish Government shall ensure that the amendments to the Constitution of Ireland set out in Annex B to the section entitled "Constitutional Issues" of the Multi-Party Agreement take effect.

In witness thereof the undersigned, being duly authorised thereto by the respective Governments, have signed this Agreement.

Done in two originals at Belfast on the 10th day of April 1998.

Tony Blair Marjorie ('Mo') Mowlam	Bertie Ahern David Andrews
For the Government of the United Kingdom of Great Britain and Northern Ireland	For the Government of Ireland

ANNEX 1

The Agreement Reached in the Multi-Party Talks

ANNEX 2

Declaration on the Provisions of Paragraph (vi) of Article 1 In Relationship to Citizenship

The British and Irish Governments declare that it is their joint understanding that the term "the people of Northern Ireland" in paragraph (vi) of Article 1 of this Agreement means, for the purposes of giving effect to this provision, all persons born in Northern Ireland and having, at the time of their birth, at least one parent who is a British citizen, an Irish citizen or is otherwise entitled to reside in Northern Ireland without any restriction on their period of residence.

PARIS PEACE ACCORD, 1973

Agreement on Ending the War and Restoring Peace in Vietnam, signed in Paris and entered into force January 17,1973.

Agreement on Ending the War and Restoring Peace in Vietnam, Signed in Paris and Entered into Force January 17, 1973

The Parties participating in the Paris Conference on Viet-Nam

With a view to ending the war and restoring peace in Viet-Nam on the basis of respect for the Vietnamese people's fundamental national rights and the South Vietnamese people's right to šelf- determination, and to contributing to the consolidation of peace in Asia and the world,

Have agreed on the following provisions and undertake to respect and to implement them:

CHAPTER-I

THE VIETNAMESE PEOPLE'S FUNDAMENTAL NATIONAL RIGHTS

Article 1

The United States and all other countries respect the independence, sovereignty, unity, and territorial integrity of Viet-Nam as recognized by the 1954 Geneva Agreements on Viet-Nam.

CHAPTER-II

CESSATION OF HOSTILITIES-WITHDRAWAL OF TROOPS

Article 2

A cease-fire shall be observed throughout South Viet-

Nam as of 2400 hours G.M.T. [Greenwich Mean Time], on January 27, 1973.

At the same hour, the United States will stop all its military activities against the territory of the Democratic Republic of Viet-Nam by ground, air and naval forces, wherever they may be based, and end the mining of the territorial waters, ports, harbors, and waterways of the Democratic Republic of Viet-Nam. The United States will remove, permanently deactivate or destroy all the mines in the territorial waters, ports, harbors, and waterways of North Viet-Nam as soon as this Agreement goes into effect.

The complete cessation of hostilities mentioned in this Article shall be durable and without limit of time.

Article 3

The parties undertake to maintain the cease-fire and to ensure a lasting and stable peace.

As soon as the cease-fire goes into effect:

(a) The United States forces and those of the other foreign countries allied with the United States and the Republic of Viet-Nam shall remain in-place pending the implementation of the pian of troop withdrawal. The Four-Party Joint Military Commission described in Article 16 shall determine the modalities.

(b) The armed forces of the two South Vietnamese parties shall remain in-place. The Two-Party Joint Military Commission described in Article 17 shall determine the areas controlled by each party and the modalities of stationing.

(c) The regular forces of all services and arms and the irregular forces of the parties in South Viet-Nam shall stop all offensive activities against each other and shall strictly abide by the following stipulations:

— All acts of force on the ground, in the air, and on the sea shall be prohibited;

— All hostile acts, terrorism and reprisals by both sides will be banned.

Article 4

The United States will not continue its military involvement or intervene in the internal affairs of South Viet-Nam.

Article 5

Within sixty days of the signing of this Agreement, there will be a total withdrawal from South Viet-Nam of troops, military advisers, and military personnel, including technical military personnel and military personnel associated with the pacification program, armaments, munitions, and war material of the United States and those of the other foreign countries mentioned in Article 3 (a). Advisers from the above-mentioned countries to all paramilitary organizations and the police force will also be withdrawn within the same period of time.

Article 6

The dismantlement of all military bases in South Viet-Nam of the United States and of the other foreign countries mentioned in Article 3 (a) shall be completed within sixty days of the signing of this agreement.

Article 7

From the enforcement of the cease-fire to the formation of the government provided for in Article, 9 (b) and 14 of this Agreement, the two South Vietnamese parties shall not accept the introduction of troops, military advisers, and military personnel including technical military personnel armaments, munitions, and war material into South Viet-Nam.

The two South Vietnamese parties shall be permitted to make periodic replacement of armaments, munitions and war material which have been destroyed, damaged, worn out or used up after the cease-fire, on the basis of piece-for-piece, of the same characteristics and properties, under the supervision of the Joint Military Commission of the two South Vietnamese parties and of the International Commission of Control and Supervision.

CHAPTER-III

THE RETURN OF CAPTURED MILITARY PERSONNEL AND FOREIGN CIVILIANS AND CAPTURED AND DETAINED VIETNAMESE CIVILIAN PERSONNEL

Article 8

(a) The return of captured military personnel and foreign civilians of the parties shall be carried out simultaneously with and completed not later than the same day as the troop withdrawal mentioned in Article 5. The parties shall exchange complete lists of the above-mentioned captured military personnel and foreign civilians on the day of the signing of this Agreement.

(b) The parties shall help each other to get information about those military personnel and foreign civilians of the parties missing in action, to determine the location and take care of the graves of the dead so as to facilitate the exhumation and repatriation of the remains, and to take any such other measures as may be required to get information about those still considered missing in action.

(c) The question of the return of Vietnamese civilian personnel captured and detained in South Viet-Nam will be resolved by the two South Vietnamese parties on the basis of the principles of Article 21 (b) of the Agreement on the Cessation of Hostilities in Viet-Nam of July 20, 1954. The two South Vietnamese parties will do so in a spirit of national reconciliation and concord, with a view to ending hatred and enmity, in order to ease suffering and to reunite families. The two South Vietnamese parties will do their utmost to resolve this question within ninety days after the cease-fire comes into effect.

CHAPTER-IV

THE EXERCISE OF THE SOUTH VIETNAMESE PEOPLE'S RIGHT TO SELF- DETERMINATION

Article 9

The Government of the United States of America and the Government of the Democratic Republic of Viet-Nam undertake to respect the following principles for the exercise of the South Vietnamese people's right to self-determination:

(a) The South Vietnamese people's right to self-determination is sacred, inalienable, and shall be respected by all countries.

(b) The South Vietnamese people shall decide themselves the political future of South Viet-Nam through genuinely free and democratic general elections under International supervision

(c) Foreign countries shall not impose any political tendency or personality on the South Vietnamese people.

Article 10

The two South Vietnamese parties undertake to respect

the cease- fire and maintain peace in South Viet-Nam, settle all matters of contention through negotiations, and avoid all armed conflict

Article 11

Immediately after the cease-fire, the two South Vietnamese parties will:

- achieve national reconciliation and concord, end hatred and enmity, prohibit all acts of reprisal and discrimination against individuals or organizations that have collaborated with one side or the other;
- ensure the democratic liberties of the people: personal freedom, freedom of speech, freedom of the press, freedom of meeting, freedom of organization, freedom of political activities, freedom of belief, freedom of movement, freedom of residence, freedom of work, right to property ownership, and right to free enterprise.

Article 12

(a) Immediately after the cease-fire, the two South Vietnamese parties shall hold consultations in a spirit of national reconciliation and concord, mutual respect, and mutual non- elimination to set up a National Council of National Reconciliation and Concord of three equal segments. The Council shall operate on the principle of unanimity, After the National Council of National Reconciliation and Concord has assumed its functions, the two South Vietnamese parties will consult about the formation of councils at lower levels. The two South Vietnamese parties shall sign an agreement on the internal matters of South Viet-Nam as soon as possible and do their utmost to accomplish this within ninety days after the cease- fire comes into effect, in keeping with the South

Vietnamese people's aspirations for peace, independence and democracy.

(b) The National Council of National Reconciliation and Concord shall have the task of promoting the two South Vietnamese parties' implementation of this Agreement, achievement of national reconciliation and concord and ensurance of democratic liberties. The National Council of National Reconciliation and Concord will organize the free and democratic general elections provided for in Article 9 (b) and decide the procedures and modalities of these general elections. The institutions for which the general elections are to be held will be agreed upon through consultations between the two South Vietnamese parties. The National Council of National Reconciliation and Concord will also decide the procedures and modalities of such local elections as the two South Vietnamese parties agree upon.

Article 13

The question of Vietnamese armed forces in South Viet-Nam shall be settled by the two South Vietnamese parties in a spirit of national reconciliation and concord, equality and mutual respect, without foreign interference, in accordance with the postwar situation. Among the questions to be discussed by the two South Vietnamese parties are steps to reduce their military effectives and to demobilize the troops being reduced. The two South Vietnamese parties will accomplish this as soon as possible.

Article 14

South Viet-Nam will pursue a foreign policy of peace and independence. It will be prepared to establish relations with all countries irrespective of their political and social systems on the basis of mutual respect for independence and sovereignty and accept economic and technical aid from any country with no political conditions attached. The acceptance of military aid by South Viet-Nam in the future shall come under the authority of the government set up after the general elections in South Viet- Nam provided for in Article 9 (b).

CHAPTER-V

THE REUNIFICATION OF VIET-NAM AND THE RELATIONSHIP BETWEEN NORTH AND SOUTH VIETNAM

Article 15

The reunification of Viet-Nam shall be carried out step by step through peaceful means on the basis of discussions and agreements between North and South Viet-Nam, without coercion or annexation by either party, and without foreign interference. The time for reunification will be agreed upon by North and South Viet-Nam-

Pending reunification:

(a) The military demarcation line between the two zones at the 17th parallel is only provisional and not a political or territorial boundary, as provided for in paragraph 6 of the Final Declaration of the 1954 Geneva Conference.

(b) North and South Viet-Nam shall respect the Demilitarized Zone on either side of the Provisional Military Demarcation Line.

(c) North and South Viet-Nam shall promptly start negotiations with a view to reestablishing-normal relations in various fields. Among the questions to be negotiated are the modalities of civilian movement across the Provisional Military Demarcation Line,

(d) North and South Viet-Nam shall not join any military alliance or military bloc and shall not allow foreign powers to maintain military bases, troops; military advisers, and military personnel on their respective territories, as stipulated in the 1954 Geneva Agreements on Viet-Nam.

CHAPTER VI

THE JOINT MILITARY COMMISSIONS, THE INTERNATIONAL COMMISSION OF CONTROL AND SUPERVISION, THE INTERNATIONAL CONFERENCE

Article 16

(a) The Parties participating in the Paris Conference on Viet- Nam shall immediately designate representatives to form a Four- Party Joint Military Commission with the task of ensuring joint action by the parties in implementing the following provisions of this Agreement:

- The first paragraph of Article 2, regarding the enforcement of the cease-fire throughout South Viet-Nam;
- Article 3 (a), regarding the cease-fire by U.S. forces and those of the other foreign countries referred to in that Article;
- Article 3 (c), regarding the cease-fire between all parties in South Viet-Nam;
- Article 5, regarding the withdrawal from South Viet-Nam of U.S. troops and those of the other foreign countries mentioned in Article 3 (a);
- Article 6, regarding the dismantlement of military bases in South Viet-Nam of the United States and those of the other foreign countries mentioned in Article 3 (a);

- Article 8 (a), regarding the return of captured military personnel and foreign civilians of the parties;
- Article 8 (b), regarding the mutual assistance of the parties in getting information about those military personnel and foreign civilians of the parties missing in action.

(b) The Four-Party Joint Military Commission shall operate in accordance with the principle of consultations and unanimity. Disagreements shall be referred to the International Commission of Control and Supervision.

(c) The Four-Party Joint Military Commission shall begin operating immediately after the signing of this Agreement and end its activities in sixty days, after the completion of the withdrawal of U.S. troops and those of the other foreign countries mentioned in Article 3 (a) and the completion of the return of captured military personnel and foreign civilians of the parties.

(d) The four parties shall agree immediately on the organization, the working procedure, means of activity, and expenditures of the Four-Party Joint Military Commission.

Article 17

(a) The two South Vietnamese parties shall immediately designate representatives to form a Two-Party Joint Military Commission with the task of ensuring joint action by the two South Vietnamese parties in implementing the following provisions of this Agreement:

- The first paragraph of Article 2, regarding the enforcement of the cease-fire throughout South Viet-Nam, when the Four-Party Joint Military Commission has ended its activities;

- Article 3 (b), regarding the cease-fire between the two South Vietnamese parties;
- Article 3 (c), regarding the cease-fire between all parties in South Viet-Nam, when the Four-Party Joint Military Commission has ended its activities;
- Article 7, regarding the prohibition of the introduction of troops into South Viet-Nam and all other provisions of this Article;
- Article 8 (c), regarding the question of the return of Vietnamese civilian personnel captured and' detained in South Viet-Nam;
- Article 1 3, regarding the reduction of the military effectives of the two South Vietnamese parties and the demobilization of the troops being reduced.

(b) Disagreements shall be referred to the International Commission of Control and Supervision.

(c) After the signing of this Agreement, the Two-Party Joint Military Commission shall agree immediately on the measures and organization aimed at enforcing the cease-fire and preserving peace in South Viet-Nam,

Article 18

(a) After the signing of this Agreement, an International Commission of Control and Supervision shall be, established immediately.

(b) Until the International Conference provided for in Article 19 makes definitive arrangements, the International Commission of Control and Supervision will report to the four parties on matters concerning the control and Supervision of the implementation of the following provisions of this Agreement:

- The first paragraph of Article 2, regarding the enforcement of the cease-fire throughout South Viet-Nam;
- Article 3 (a), regarding the cease-fire by U.S. forces and those of the other foreign countries referred to in that Article;
- Article 3 (c), regarding the cease-fire between all the parties in South Viet-Nam;
- Article 5, regarding the withdrawal from South Viet-Nam of U.S. troops and those of the other foreign countries mentioned in Article 3 (a),
- Article 6, regarding the dismantlement of military bases in South Viet-Nam of the United States and those of the other foreign countries mentioned in Article 3 (a);
- Article 8 (a), regarding the return of captured military personnel and foreign civilians of the parties.

The International Commission of Control and Supervision shall form control teams for carrying out its tasks. The four parties shall agree immediately on the location and operation of these teams. The parties will facilitate their operation.

(c) Until the International Conference makes definitive arrangements, the International Commission of control and Supervision will report to the two South Vietnamese parties on matters concerning the control and supervision of the implementation of the following provisions of this Agreement:

- The first paragraph of Article 2, regarding the enforcement of the cease-fire throughout South Viet-

Nam, when the Four-Party Joint Military Commission has ended its activities;

- Article 3 (b), regarding the cease-fire between the two South Vietnamese parties;
- Article 3 (c), regarding the cease-fire between all parties in South Viet-Nam, when the Four-Party Joint Military Commission has ended its activities;
- Article 7, regarding the prohibition of the introduction of troops into South Viet-Nam and all other provisions of this Article;
- Article 8 (c), regarding the question of the return of Vietnamese civilian personnel captured and detained in South Viet-Nam;
- Article 9 (b), regarding the free and democratic general elections in South Viet-Nam;
- Article 13, regarding the reduction of the military effectives of the two South Vietnamese parties and the demobilization of the troops being reduced,

The International Commission of Control and Supervision shall form control teams for carrying out its tasks. The two South Vietnamese parties shall agree immediately on the location and operation of these teams. The two South Vietnamese parties will facilitate their operation.

(d) The International Commission of Control and Supervision shall be composed of representatives of four countries: Canada, Hungary, Indonesia and Poland. The chairmanship of this Commission will rotate among the members for specific periods to be determined by the Commission.

(e) The International Commission of Control and Supervision shall carry out its tasks in accordance with the principle of respect for the sovereignty of South Viet-Nam.

(f) The International Commission of Control and Supervision shall operate in accordance with the principle of consultations and unanimity.

(g) The International Commission of Control and Supervision shall begin operating when a cease-fire comes into force in Viet-Nam. As regards the provisions in Article 18 (b) concerning the four parties, the International Commission of Control and Supervision shall end its activities when the Commission's tasks of control and supervision regarding these provisions have been fulfilled. As regards the provisions in Article 18 (c) concerning the two South Vietnamese parties, the International Commission of Control and Supervision shall end its activities on the request of the government formed after the general elections in South Viet-Nam provided for in Article 9 (b).

(h) The four parties shall agree immediately on the organization, means of activity, and expenditures of the International Commission of Control and Supervision. The relationship between the International Commission and the International Conference will be agreed upon by the International Commission and the International Conference.

Article 19

The parties agree on the convening of an International Conference within thirty days of the signing of this Agreement to acknowledge the signed agreements; to guarantee the ending of the war, the maintenance of peace in Viet-Nam, the respect of the Vietnamese people's fundamental national rights, and the South Vietnamese people's right to self-determination; and to contribute to and guarantee peace in Indochina.

The United States and the Democratic Republic of Viet-Nam, on behalf of the parties participating in the Paris Conference on Viet-Nam will propose to the following parties that they participate in this International Conference: the People's Republic of China, the Republic of France, the Union of Soviet Socialist Republics, the United Kingdom, the four countries of the International Commission of Control and Supervision, and the Secretary General of the United Nations, together with the parties participating in the Paris Conference on Viet-Nam.

CHAPTER VII
REGARDING CAMBODIA AND LAOS

Article 20

(a) The parties participating in the Paris Conference on Viet- Nam shall strictly respect the 1954 Geneva Agreements on Cambodia's and the 1954 Geneva Agreements on Laos, which recognized the Cambodian and the Lao peoples' fundamental national rights, i.e., the independence, sovereignty, unity, and territorial integrity of these countries. The parties shall respect the neutrality of Cambodia and Laos.

The parties participating in the Paris Conference on Viet-Nam undertake to refrain from using the territory of Cambodia and the territory of Laos to encroach on the sovereignty and security of one another and of other countries.

(b) Foreign countries shall put an end to all military activities in Cambodia and Laos, totally withdraw from and refrain from reintroducing into these two countries troops, military advisers and military personnel, armaments, munitions and war material.

(c) The internal affairs of Cambodia and Laos shall be settled by the people of each of these countries without foreign interference.

(d) The problems existing between the Indochinese countries shall be settled by the Indochinese parties on the basis of respect for each other's independence, sovereignty, and territorial integrity, and non-interference in each other's internal affairs.

CHAPTER VIII

THE RELATIONSHIP BETWEEN THE UNITED STATES AND THE DEMOCRATIC REPUBLIC OF VIETNAM

Article 21

The United States anticipates that this Agreement will usher in an era of reconciliation with the Democratic Republic of Viet- Nam as with all the peoples of Indochina. In pursuance of its traditional policy, the United States will contribute to healing the wounds of war and to postwar reconstruction of the Democratic Republic of Viet-Nam and throughout Indochina.

Article 22

The ending of the war, the restoration of peace in Viet-Nam, and the strict implementation of this Agreement will create conditions for establishing a new, equal and mutually beneficial relationship between the United States and the Democratic Republic of Viet-Nam on the basis of respect for each other's independence and sovereignty, and non-interference in each other's internal affairs. At the same time this will ensure stable peace in Viet-Nam and contribute to the preservation of lasting peace in Indochina and Southeast Asia.

CHAPTER IX

OTHER PROVISIONS

Article 23

This Agreement shall enter into force upon signature by plenipotentiary representatives of the parties participating in the Paris Conference on Viet-Nam. All the parties concerned shall strictly implement this Agreement and its Protocols. Done in Paris this twenty-seventh day of January, one thousand nine hundred and seventy-three, in English and Vietnamese. The English and Vietnamese texts are official and equally authentic.

For the Government of
The United States of America
(Signed):
William P. Rogers
Secretary of State

For the Government of
The Republic of Vietnam
(Signed):
Tran Van Lam
Minister for Foreign Affairs

FOR THE GOVERNMENT
OF THE DEMOCRATIC
REPUBLIC OF VIETNAM:

(Signed):
Nguyen Duy Trinh
Minister for Foreign Affairs

FOR THE PROVISIONAL
REVOLUTIONARY GOVERN-
MENT OF THE REPUBLIC OF
SOUTH VIET-NAM:
(Signed):
Nguyen Thi Binh
Minister for Foreign Affairs

OSLO II AGREEMENT

Washington, DC, September 28, 1995

ISRAELI-PALESTINIAN INTERIM AGREEMENT ON THE WEST BANK AND THE GAZA STRIP

The Government of the State of Israel and the Palestine Liberation Organization (hereinafter "the PLO"), the representative of the Palestinian people;

Preamble

Within the framework of the Middle East peace process initiated at Madrid in October 1991:

Reaffirming their determination to put an end to decades of confrontation and to live in peaceful coexistence, mutual dignity and security, while recognizing their mutual legitimate and political rights;

Reaffirming their desire to achieve a just, lasting and comprehensive peace settlement and historic reconciliation through the agreed political process;

Recognizing that the peace process and the new era that it has created, as well as the new relationship established between the two Parties as described above, are irreversible, and the determination of the two Parties to maintain, sustain and continue the peace process;

Recognizing that the aim of the Israeli-Palestinian negotiations within the current Middle East peace process is, among other things, to establish a Palestinian Interim Self-Government Authority, i.e. the elected Council (hereinafter "the Council" or "the Palestinian Council"), and the elected Ra'ees of the Executive Authority, for the Palestinian people in the West Bank and the Gaza Strip, for a transitional period not exceeding five years from the date of signing the Agreement on the Gaza Strip and the Jericho Area (hereinafter "the Gaza-Jericho Agreement") on May 4, 1994, leading to a permanent settlement based on Security Council Resolutions 242 and 338;

Reaffirming their understanding that the interim self-government arrangements contained in this Agreement are an integral part of the whole peace process, that the negotiations on the permanent status, that will start as soon as possible but not later than May 4, 1996, will lead to the implementation of Security Council Resolutions 242 and 338, and that the Interim Agreement shall settle all the issues of the interim period and that no such issues will be deferred to the agenda of the permanent status negotiations;

Reaffirming their adherence to the mutual recognition and commitments expressed in the letters dated September 9, 1993, signed by and exchanged between the Prime Minister of Israel and the Chairman of the PLO;

Desirous of putting into effect the Declaration of Principles on Interim Self-Government Arrangements signed at Washington, D.C. on September 13, 1993, and the Agreed Minutes thereto (hereinafter "the DOP") and in particular Article III and Annex I concerning the holding of direct, free and general political elections for the Council and the Ra'ees of the Executive Authority in order that the Palestinian people in the West Bank, Jerusalem and the Gaza Strip may democratically elect accountable representatives:

Recognizing that these elections will constitute a significant interim preparatory step toward the realization of the legitimate rights of the Palestinian people and their just requirements and will provide a democratic basis for the establishment of Palestinian institutions;

Reaffirming their mutual commitment to act, in accordance with this Agreement, immediately, efficiently and effectively against acts or threats of terrorism, violence or incitement, whether committed by Palestinians or Israelis;

Following the Gaza- Jericho Agreement; the Agreement on Preparatory Transfer of Powers and Responsibilities signed at Erez on August 29, 1994 (hereinafter "the Preparatory Transfer Agreement"); and the Protocol on Further Transfer of Powers and Responsibilities signed at Cairo *on* August 1995 (hereinafter "the Further Transfer Protocol"); which three agreements will be superseded by this Agreement;

HEREBY AGREE as follows:

CHAPTER 1: THE COUNCIL

Article 1

Transfer of Authority

1. Israel shall transfer powers and responsibilities as specified in this Agreement from the Israeli military government and its Civil Administration to the Council in accordance with this Agreement. Israel shall continue to exercise powers and responsibilities not so transferred.

2. Pending the inauguration of the Council, the powers and responsibilities transferred to the Council shall be exercised by the Palestinian Authority established in accordance with the Gaza-Jericho Agreement, which shall also have all the rights, liabilities and obligations to be assumed by the Council in this regard. Accordingly, the term "Council" throughout this Agreement shall, pending the inauguration of the Council, be construed as meaning the Palestinian Authority.

3. The transfer of powers and responsibilities to the

police force established by the Palestinian Council in accordance with Article XIV below (hereinafter "the Palestinian Police") shall be accomplished in a phased manner, as detailed in this Agreement and in the Protocol concerning Redeployment and Security Arrangements attached as Annex I to this Agreement.

4. As regards the transfer and assumption of authority in civil spheres, powers and responsibilities shall be transferred and assumed as set out in the Protocol Concerning Civil Affairs attached as Annex III to this Agreement (hereinafter "Annex III").

5. After the inauguration of the Council, the Civil Administration in the West Bank will be dissolved, and the Israeli military government shall be withdrawn. The withdrawal of the military government shall not prevent it from exercising the powers and responsibilities not transferred to the Council.

6. A Joint Civil Affairs Coordination and Cooperation Committee (hereinafter "the C AE"), Joint Regional Civil Affairs Subcommittees, one for the Gaza Strip and the other for the West Bank, and District Civil Liaison Offices in the West Bank shall be established in order to provide for coordination and cooperation in civil affairs between the Council and Israel, as" detailed in Annex III.

7. The offices of the Council, and the offices of its Ra'ees and its Executive Authority and other committees, shall be located in areas under Palestinian territorial jurisdiction in the West Bank and the Gaza Strip.

Article II

Elections

1. In order that the Palestinian people of the West

Bank and the Gaza Strip may govern themselves according to democratic principles, direct, free and general political elections will be held for the Council and the Ra'ees of the Executive Authority of the Council in accordance with the provisions set out in the Protocol concerning Elections attached as Annex II to this Agreement (hereinafter "Annex II").

2. These elections will constitute a significant interim preparatory step towards the realization of the legitimate rights of the Palestinian people and their just requirements and will provide a democratic basis for the establishment of Palestinian institutions.

3. Palestinians of Jerusalem who live there may participate in the election process in accordance with the provisions contained in this Article and in Article VI of Annex II (Election Arrangements concerning Jerusalem).

4. The elections shall be called by the Chairman of the Palestinian Authority immediately following the signing of this Agreement to take place at the earliest practicable date following the redeployment of Israeli forces in accordance with Annex I, and consistent with the requirements of the election timetable as provided in Annex II, the Election Law and the Election Regulations, as defined in Article I of Annex II.

* * * * * * *

The two Parties view the West Bank and the Gaza Strip as a single territorial unit, the integrity and status of which will be preserved during the interim period.

The PLO undertakes that, within two months of the date of the inauguration of the Council, the Palestinian National Council will convene and formally approve the necessary changes in regard to the Palestinian Covenant, as undertaken in the letters signed by the Chairman of the PLO and addressed to the Prime Minister of Israel, dated September 9, 1993 and May 4, 1994

Pursuant to Annex I, Article IX of this Agreement, Israel confirms that the permanent checkpoints on the roads leading to and from the Jericho Area (except those related to the access road leading from Mousa Alami to the Allenby Bridge) will be removed upon the completion of the first phase of redeployment.

Prisoners who, pursuant to the Gaza-Jericho Agreement, were turned over to the Palestinian Authority on the condition that they remain in the Jericho Area for the remainder of their sentence, will be free to return to their homes in the West Bank and the Gaza Strip upon the completion of the first phase of redeployment.

As regards relations between Israel and the PLO, and without derogating from the commitments contained in the letters signed by and exchanged between the Prime Minister of Israel and the Chairman of the PLO, dated September 9, 1993 and May 4, 1994, the two sides will apply between them the provisions contained in Article XXII, paragraph l, with the necessary changes.

- The Preamble to this Agreement, and all Annexes, Appendices and maps attached hereto, shall constitute an integral part hereof.
- The Parties agree that the maps attached to the Gaza-Jericho Agreement as:
    1. map No. l (The Gáza Strip), an exact copy of which is attached to this Agreement as map No. (in this Agreement "map No. 2");
    2. map No. 4 (Deployment of Palestinian Police

in the Gáza Strip), an exact copy of which is attached to this Agreement as map No. 5 (in this Agreement "map No. 5"); and

3. map No. 6 (Maritime Activity Zones), an exact copy of which is attached to this Agreement as map No. 8 (in this Agreement "map No. 8"; are an integral part hereof and will remain in effect for the duration of this Agreement.

While the Jeftlik area will come under the functional and personal jurisdiction of the Council in the first phase of redeployment, the area's transfer to the territorial jurisdiction of the Council will be considered by the Israeli side in the first phase of the further redeployment phases.

Done at Washington DC, this 28th day of September, 1995.
For the Government of the State of Israel:
For the PLO:
Witnessed by:
The United States of America
The Russian Federation
The Arab Republic of Egypt
The Hashemite Kingdom of Jordan
The Kingdom of Norway
The European Union

ex 1 - Redeployment and Security Arrangements
ex 2 - Elections Protocol
ex 3 - Civil Affairs
ex 4 - Legal Matters
ex 5 - Economic Relations
ex 6 - Israeli-Palestinian Cooperation
ex 7 - Release of Palestinian Prisoners
No. 1 - First Phase of Redeployment (A & B)
No. 2 - Security Arrangements in the Gáza Strip
No. 5 - Palestinian Police Deployment - Gáza
No. 6 - Safe Passage Routes
No. 8 - Maritime Activity Zones
No. 9 - Hebron

8

Early National Institutions (NE Region)

The NE region has a legacy of several early institutions. We choose one. The nation-state of Manipur had successfully evolved civilizational values, principles of constitutionalism, rule of law and justice during its two millennia of historical experience within the monarchical and feudalistic framework, which obviously bore the testimony of inevitable, institutional arrogance and brutality. The valley Meetei herrenvolk had crafted a confederacy of several independent principalities with relatively autonomous village republics of Meetei-cognate tribes, which had been known to the British as Manipuri Nagas and Manipuri Kukis. Manipuri civilization in a broad sense of the term had been multicultural and pluralistic.

The valley people had a royal edict on criminal law in 429 A.D., a constitutional system since 1100 A.D. along with tribal customary law and justicing sub-systems. The national institutions Lallup, Shinglup, Cheirap, Khulbu and, Khullakpa, among others, remained the cornerstone of Manipuri civil society and state till the British intervention in the late 19th century. Certain values endure in the Manipuri civil society after weeding out some others due to obsolescence rendered by the imposing modern institutions.

Structural Engineers in the Past

People of Manipur — the Manipuris in brief--had crafted the Manipuri history in the way history had ever been made out of scattered human groups in Europe or, India or elsewhere after the first settlers from South-East Asia had occupied the space and time. The herrenvolk Meeteis and the peripheral Meetei-cognate tribes moulded the confederal and pluralistic history within the territory of the state through violent as well as friendly interactions in varying degrees. Manipuri kings viz., Nongda Lairel Pakhangba of the Ningthouja elan, Loiyamba, Kiyamba, Khagemba, and Pamheiba, among others, had built up national institutions — political, socio-economic, cultural, constitutional, legal in progression. King Kangba — a king who preceded Pakhangba in proto-historical period had accepted Sarish (Sanamahi) as the almighty of the Meeteis, did a little bit of homework in the Meetei ethnogenesis. The thirty Manipuri hill tribes — the Meetei cognates scattered in the high altitude areas of the present state, who were given Naga and Kuki nomenclatures by the British not so long ago in Manipur history, for the colonial convenience only managed their primordial form of village republics with their Khullakpas (Ningthous or village chiefs) as their respective political and cultural authority while retaining the community land in tact and customary laws, which are sometimes democratic or authoritarian in varying degrees.

With their relative village autonomy, the Meetei - cognate tribes remain the inalienable part and parcel of Manipuri history inspite of the recent imperialistic policies of certain expansionist groups in the region. They evolved their own autonomous form of legal sub-systems, civil and criminal justicing systems, several of which are retained even today. Institutions like hero worship through head hunting, inter-clan blood feuds had been weeded out by the Christian principles and modern institutions.

The centralized Meetei confederacy, later transformed into Manipur state had evolved a centralized administration after assimilating seven independent kingdoms, created a central market, institutionalized a monarchical polity equipped with state apparatus (Loishangs — i.e. government departments), defence apparatus and a foreign ministry (Awapurel), Territorial consolidation followed by Panna classification, land laws, taxation system had been completed in phases. A penal code had been adopted in 429 A.D., to be followed by the adoption of a Constitution in 1100 A.D.. National institutions had developed in the Manipuri body polity thereby evolving civilizational values, constitutionalism, rule of law, criminal laws, land laws, judicial and justicing system.

Some racist scholars made a point that after the valley Meeteis converted to Vaishnavism, the Hindu stalwarts and the British intruders had civilized the savage. This is a misnomer and prejudicial concoction. The Chinese called the white people and westerners barbarian and savage. It also happens other way round. Manipuri polity had successfully crafted national institutions like the basic laws, criminal laws and other mechanisms in the last two millennia of struggle for survival and ascendancy.

Dissent against authoritarianism: The early Manipuri polity had been structurally authoritarian because of the monarchical institution as it had been elsewhere. However, the testimony of active dissent bore proven democratic values, which survive even today in the changed context and epoch.The early Manipuri text- **Numit Kappa** is a narrative of class struggle of an oppressed individual slave against two ruling Manipuri kings (Numit i.e. sun).

The elder of the two suns (read kings) had been shot down by arrow of the slave, whereas the younger king in his cowardly style led away from the kingdom out of the fear of a committed Manipuri slave. An extract from the narrative:

> *Khuwaai Nongchongpam Naicha Yekma Haotangla Namu Pongparacha Atanpana. ... Tauhuireng Ahanpapapu soiyonle. ...Nawa khoichu tenna. ...yimu phiraksana. ... trau tau kapthare. ...SanaKhommaton Atonpa. ...Lairen makonnungta santhupkhire Loiren khunpilokta.*

The Numit Kappa legacy had not been disapproved by the Manipuri citizens of the early period and the legacy had passed onto the new generations. The eminent principles like—"Leibakna Namma Ningthouna Namma "(king on one side and the people on another side) and" Ningthou ngamba Angamba" (noblemen who can win over the king. Ningthou Pongba Tara" (ten noble men who function alongside the king) had evolved ovìø the centuries notwithstanding the authoritarian monarchy. Thonglen of the Moirang principality is one such nobleman who proves equal to the might of the king.

The rebel thought had been demonstrated by not less than seven royal scholars who resisted the king in the 18th century. One of the rebel scholars Moirnag Lalhanba had been thrown into the burning stacks by the servants of the king. Frequent uprisings and insurgencies both from the plain areas and the Manipur hills contested — seat of power in a routine manner.

The 1947 Manipur State Constitution of sovereign Manipur banned awarding of capital punishment to political dissenters and political rebels. The deeply engrained rebel thought and dissent philosophy softened the rigours of the institutional authoritarianism. Democratic values had been seeded in early Manipur. Active dissent is an early political convention of the Manipuri civil society which hierarchical or caste-based society would hardly perceive in its imagining ability.

Certain evidence or relics of anti-authoritarian conscience-structure could be witnessed even today. Iromchanu Sharmila's six year old fasting against AFSPA, 1958 leaves far behind any fasting human being or, leader elsewhere irrespective of the stature or political cause advanced. Self-immolation of a Manipuri youth — Pebam Chittaranjan against AFSPA and similar other contemporary forms of dissent are apparently relics of Numit Kappa allegory. Certain values still survive in spite of great institutional changes. Several other democratic forms of dissent are visible in a routine manner.

12th Century Manipuri Constitutionalism

Manipuri constitutionalism, rule of law and established justicing system could be traced to Manipuri Constitution — Loiyamba Shinyen, adopted by the king Loiyamba in 1100 A.D. Royal edict on Manipuri Penal Code had been adopted in 429 A.D., in a rudimentary form. Manipuri hill tribes had their own relatively autonomous sub-systems which vary from village to village- each village functioning as republic with the least intervention in their domestic affairs from the Manipur king whose main administration and seat of central authority lies in the valley. The national institution of Lallup — a military organization had been set up in the early period, probably during the reign of Nongda Lairen Pakhangba in 33 A.D.

It had been closed down due to the British disarmament of the Manipuris since 1891. The national institution of Shinglup- a civil society, village level mechanism had been found to be equally old. The institution as such exists no more save the spirit of Shinglup that glues the civil society even today in another context.

SHINGLUP is an important civil society organization, constituted under the leadership of the village chief. Literally, it means Shing(woods)- Lup (organization). When a man dies in the village, woods are collected for the funeral of the deceased. In functional terms, it transcends the funeral matter. In small disputes, the Shinglup amicably decides the issue and maintains the village solidarity. In economic terms, as and when some one is sick, assistance is given to the sick; and food is served to extremely needy family in trying times. In some cases, houses had been constructed with the village assistance. The spirit of the national institution has been found till the other day in the recent past.

LALLUP is the most important defence, or military organization in the realm functioning for nearly two millennia till the British interventionists in Manipur sovereignty abolished it, in order to militarily immobilize the Manipuris, under a false pretext of modernizing the pre-modern Manipuri polity. British writers had a bad opinion of this institution by comparaing it with forced labour and not with the western practice of Conscription. Service to the state for defence is what the institution stands for.

The institution functions as a military organization with Lalmee (soldier), Lallupchnigba (leader of the militia) and Khundin -the supervisor of the institution as the military resources and assets. A militia member has to render 10 days service free in 40 days. In peacetime, the soldier-members of the institution serve the state (read king) in different civil capacities like bridge construction, road construction, craftsmanship or leatherwork. The British considered it as forced labour; however ,defence of the realm in as many as six pannahs (valley division) was found necessary. Every male of the age group 17 to 60 barring women, sickmen, oldmen above the age of 60, Peebas(clan heads) had been drawn from the Meeteis, the Manipuri Brahmins and Muslims to the military service.

A lalmee (soldier) in the institution has been entitled to cultivate one pari (2 and a half acres) of cultivable land subject to payment of tax to the state. In case of illness, a substitute has to be sent or a fine of one rupee has to be paid. The supervisors do not deposit the fine to the state, and deposit to their pockets. Even to-day the legacy continues.

After the abolition of Lallup, land revenue of Rs. 4/ for each pari has been collected and it has been raised to Rs. 5/ later on. The lakpas, who collected the revenues got 10% of his collections. Paradoxically, some officials in the present state expect to receive some commission from, the citizens. Some call it corruption, but the officials are found to be very honest in the said deal. The institution makes hole for unscrupulous people in power.

In Manipur hill areas, five hill divisions — Lam viz., Tangkhul lam, Mao lam, Kapui lam, Tammu lam and Moirang lam have been made and placed under lam subadars. A house tax of Rs. 3 has been collected in the late 1890s from every Manipuri hill house. The division of the lams does not plant the seeds of inaccessible ethnic homelands; it is rather a suitable mechanism for revenue collection under British days.

The state and territory has remained in tact inspite of the internal trappings devised for revenue matters only. At a point of time, the seven independent valley principalities had separate territories which had to melt away towards forming a common and shared territory. The imagined and projected ethnic homelands of today in modern Manipur, particularly after 1947, is a part of contemporary political mobilization.

Early Justice System

Early Manipuri theory and mechanisms of justice has been characterized by divine ordeals, natural mandates to be followed by positivist, constitutional and legal devices. The feudalism and monarchicalism like their universal counterparts in the west and the east remains the overarching pinnacle of justice. The king remains the law-giver and fountainhead of justice whereas, he has never been different from any other human beings.

Citizens owe responsibilities to the state and his or her civil liberties remain extension of the responsibilities. The significance of justice as fairness has been arbitrary, although the noblemen — the feudal order has rendered the justice system to be fair exclusively to them. As regards the separation of powers, judiciary has been separate from the executive, but the boundary remains blurred. An extract from the royal edict in 429 A.D.:

> *Meidingu Apanbana wahei ani haipharoi...Kaidanaba wayen chumo, thoutha namguno....Thakshikhasi Namlanguno... Wayel kaipharoiye...Ninghtou shemba Meeshingdee tumna hato* wayen chumo means do proper justice)

During king Kangba's period, each of the two opponent parties seeking justice has to plant a flag before each of them. The party whose flag falls down due to the wind is the loser of the justice. Ordeal by fire and also by water have been prevalent. Gradually, the Manipuri judiciary crystallized into (1) the king as the ultimate appellate authority, (2) the **Cheirap** — the Supreme Court of the land with hereditary judges; (3) the **Top Garod** — the military court for trial of soldiers and defence personnels,

(4) the **Pacha** — court for the women only and (5) minor courts including court for trial of persons injuring the cattle, the Shinglup, among others. The Manipuri hillmen — the Meetei-cognates, recently renamed as Manipuri Nagas and Manipuri Kukis to suit the British colonial interests, have their own near autonomous village-level judiciary under the Khullakpas-chiefs. When the British interventionist comes, their offenders staying in Manipur state have been tried differently with the British officials in the chair. Kazi administered to the Manipuri Muslims. Women and Manipuri Brahmins have been spared from being awarded capital punishment. In contemporary justicing this immunity is indefensible.

The penal system was not refined and crude like the early British crudities in their own homeland. **Chatlam Lutin** is the manual for laws regulating sexual misconducts. Treason and murder has been awarded with capital punishment. Flogging, packing rebel princes in the bag and throwing into deep rivers, humiliation of women offender in public (Khong-goinaba), exile of delinquents to Sugnu (Sugnu-loithaba), degradation of offenders to the Loi areas, imposition of fine, among others, are common forms of punishment. The royal edicts which provide the penal code have been revised. The royal chronicle **Cheitharol Kumbaba** records punishments meted out to offenders.

Two institutions are infamous and malignant. The **Churanthaba** like the present day commandos abduct people for sacrifice to non-existent deities. There is sanction of the king behind this nefarious institution. Mild form of slavery has existed in Manipur till it has been abolished in the 20th century. These two institutions have been weeded out. One notable feature is that Manipuri women enjoy more liberties than their western counterparts, who are struggling with liberation movement even today. 'Media Paibis' are active in civil society.

Meenai - a mild form of slavery existed in two forms-voluntary slavery as in the case of debtor remaining in the house of the creditor till settlement of the debt has been made; involuntary slavery as in the case of an offender remaining by rendering services to the king. A thief has to remain a slave till the recovery of the goods is made or, in the case of adultery, the offender remaining as slave till the damages he owes for the offence has been cleared.

Unlike the European or British models of barbaric and dehumanising slavery in the past or even the caste brutality as India nurtured for millennia by the self-righteous non-repentent high caste Talibans, Manipuri form of nominal slavery would retain the slave as a part of the family he or she resides in by co-working with the family members of the owner. The slave cannot be mistreated or dishonoured. In the event of a slave fleeing away from a home, the owner is blamed for his misconduct with the slave. Ironically, some people take money form some other and offers himself as a slave in order to get the easy food, clothes and amenities. British writers impute this form of slavery to laziness.

The king had three kinds of slaves. The **Ayokpa** (or the adopted one) is the major class, who have been treated fondly. In rarest of rare case, cruelty has been meted out to slaves thereby inviting public attention to the cruelty. The nefarious institution has been weeded out, by the modem institutions. Any form of slavery -American or Manipuri — brutal or mild whatsoever — is indefensible by any Socratic method or argument. Monarchy has never been good to the valley Meeteis or the Meetei -cognates in the hills (now known as Nagas or Kukis to the British colonial jargon). The political institution of monarchy has been dead, and rejected by history in Manipur. Some primitive feudal elements however, imagine that the dead institution exists in another form in the republican epoch of humanity.

Inter-Civilization Dialogue

Manipuri civilization itself represents intra-civilizational dialogue within a constricted spatial time frame, among the Sinic, the Indian and the native Manipuri civilizational partners. Manipuri national institutions are the physical embodiment of articulated historical experiences spreading over from primordialism to contemporary multi-culturalism, tilting towards Orientalism.

The law and justice structure reflects the native achievements through trial and error. As usual, history is a glorification of a national past- apparent or partially real by overlooking the weakness and failures of all kinds. Manipur has not been an exception to this universal rule. The influences given by the British and the Hindusthan to the early institutions provides a dialectical upgradation of the institutions and in the process, unsustainable institutions like monarchy and slavery etc. have faded away.

Certain aspects of the Manipuri thought, values, principles and axiological structures could, however, survive. These sustained values have to be addressed to in any process involving intra-civilizational dialogue, which itself happens to be inalienable in a never- ending time travel of the civil society.

FURTHER READING

1. N. Sanajaoba, ed., *Manipur: Past and Present* vol I (1988), II, III and IV (2005). *Manipur: A British Anthology*, vols. I.

2. Manipur, *Treaties and Documents,* vol. I, 1993.
3. O. Bhogeshwar, *Loina Shinlon*, 1967.
4. Khullem Chandrashekhar, *Loyyamba Shinyen*, 1975.
5. do, Masil, 1997.
6. Laishram Nityai, *Ningthou Kangparol...*, 1982.
7. M. McCulloh, *Valley of Manipur*, 1859.
8. R. Brown, *Statistical Account of Manipur*, 1874.
9. E.W. Dun, *Gazetteer of Manipur*, 1886.
10. T.C. Hodson, *The Meitheis*, 1908.
11. do, *The Naga Tribes of Manipur*, 1911.
12. B.C. Allen, Naga hills and Manipur, 1905.
13. Gangmumei Kabui, *History of Manipur*, vol. I, 1991.
14. L. Ibungohal and N. Khelchandra, ed., *Cheitharol Kumbaba*, 1967.

Annex

ON GREATER HOMELAND DEMANDS*

GO—How do you describe the indigenous situation in the world and in India in particular?

Prof. N. Sanajaoba: The 20th century marks the end of imperialism in the first stage, fascism in the second stage and termination of colonialism in the third stage. The 21st century world order should be any thinking on some of the incomplete and unfinished agenda of the global family, the humanity. There are some national; questions, which are yet to be addressed to. There are Nearly 60 people or nations (which) want to form Nation States. How far will they be able to complete the entire agenda with the approval of the International community, or the United Nations. It is yet to be seen.

Secondly, there are well-established multi-national or Nation-states, which contain substantial number of minorities. These minorities rights have to be fully addressed to in these established, well-recognised Nation-states or multi-Nation states or Federations. It is more so in Africa and also in Asia. Regarding Europe and America, these matters have already been settled but even today in USA Indigenous-related issues remain. Sermething is in Canada. As far as Asia is concerned, there are some issues, which

---

* Interview with *Grassroots Options* journal, Shillong, Autumn, 2001.

have to be addressed. For example, Kashmir, Assam, Manipur, Nagaland, Tripura in India, Tibet in China. Chechnya in Russia, Tamil issue in Sri Lanka and Taiwan-China relationship. These are some of the unfinished agenda.

Regarding the indigenous issues world over, the Indigenous Peoples' Forum has come into existence with the approval of ECOSOC of the UN. It may become a reality by the end of this year or next year. Indigenous Peoples' voices have to be heard and addressed to. It's a totally new perspective in the world, order. Now, question arises in regards to the indigenous issues and minority rights. Normally, indigenous people are minority but all the minorities need not be indigenous. We have to be very careful, while making distinction between the minorities and the indigenous (people's) rights. We have to go by benchmark of the United Nations forum or the national standards responses should conform as far as possible to the global standard or UN standard. Another major issue is about re-colonisation and the new world economic disorder. Re-colonisation is happening, may be through Intellectual power, may be through trade relations or political re-colonisation; re-colonisation specially occurs in the third and the fourth world.

The new world order though considered to be very good, looking at the way things are moving on it looks like a world disorder in terms of economic relationship. Some people are quite happy with WTO and many other economic arrangements, but the Breton wood Institutions, which are imperialistic in nature, have not changed substantially. Indian leaders also simply adjusted to the demand from their friendly countries like America so that America's requirement may be considered as India's requirement where as vice-versa it may not be true. So, the new world order "especially the econonic order, to me seems to be a new world disorder. There may be economic boom in some sectors but 90 per cent of the world populution is still suffering from malnutrition, hunger and poverty.

GO—How is this going to affect the small communities of the northeast who neither have political clout nor economic power?

Regarding the North-Eastern states, communities or nationalities, whatever may be the term, it's a question of political linguistics. Someone may prefer to call it sub-nationality but I call it nationality. And instead of using the term "tribes," I would prefer to use the term "micro-nationalities". Because tribal state in any human evolution is always transitory no community can remain tribal forever. It's a process of elevating oneself to nationhood. 'Tribal states cannot be permanent things. They can form themselves into nationhood by developing common language common economic basis or common political programme. I don't feel happy, when our communities in the Northeast, always prefer to remain as "tribal" states; they should try to transform themselves into nationhood. This is one question.

Secondly the north eastern communities in one sense have been different from the mainstream Indians because of unique historical experience they had. For example, Assam did not become a part of British India till the Yandabo Treaty in 1826 coming to force. Assam, however, was not a party to the Yandabo treaty signed between the British and Burma. So there is some lacuna.

Thirdly, Manipur and Tripura were independent, princely states. Then Nagaland, specially the Naga hill districts at *a* particular point of time, did administration and independent of Indian administration. The Mizos, if one strictly interprets the foreigners' law, have been the latest immigrants and in one sense, they're of Burmese origin. However, through a process of Accord between the Mizo rebels and the Indian government they have been allowed to form a state within India. Geographically the north-eastern states have links with the mainstream through a very slender Siliguri neck.

Secondly by and large the north-eastern people, and many of them are of Austric, Mongolian and Australoid groups although Caucasian strains were seen. But predominantly they are Mongolian people. Whereas the mainland India constitutes very little of Mongoloid population, virtually nil. Mongolian people are not by race inferior people. But they are considered as stigma by the mainland India. This has given some sort of slur in the mindset of north-eastern people. That's why when these two groups — mainland people and the north-eastern people — meet each other, instinctively they cannot develop the harmonious relations. They look down upon the north-eastern people. So, how can they constitute a nation? In political linguistics, they are distinct political groups. Therefore, some outfits want to exercise their right to self determination; they want to be independent states. They want to be UN members.

The northeast mind has been very much alienated from the mainstrem thinking. This by and large is the contribution of rules in Delhi not only economically socially, culturally but even racially they have contributed to the total alienation of the north-eastern people. Ironically, the Government of India has not given economic infrastructure in the last 50 years to the Northeast. It still thinks, this the northeast is nobody's land and projects India as a geographical expression, and not a totality of economic, socio-cultural expression. The GOI also wants to use the military means.

For 50 years, they have done so to subjugate people, but they have utterly failed to militarily contain the agitation, protests and the movements. It should be wise enough to see that solution can be founs like the case of East Timor, Namibia, Western Sahara, Puerto Rico etc, This type of solution may be considered by the Indian government. But militarily, it's a futile exercise. Its counter-productive and they've given a bad name to humanity. And unless the political solution is resolved, economically these people cannot grow up the Northeast is that political subjugation should be terminated now. This is how I feel.

GO—India has entered ceasefire both with Kashmiri and Naga militants. Do you see any shift in the Indian policy?

Well, as a curious student of a social science, I do honestly feel that these two issues -- Kashmir issue and the northeast issue cannot be treated on par. Regarding Kashmir issues, the permanent factor is Pakistan a foreign country claiming Kashmir and UN resolutions since 1947 till 57, they always involved Pakistan as a co-factor with India to decide the Kashmir issue. The third country factor is totally missing in the north-east India. So, if the Kashmir issue was to be amicably resolved, no Government of India can abandon Pakistan. Three parties were always involved from the very beginning since Nehru's letter to the Security Council.

On the other hand the northeastern people/states themselves constitute an independent party. If they have to come to negotiating table, no third party is involved, except in the case of a guarantor, they may require a

Super Power or UN as a mediator. Otherwise no third country has a vital national interest in the northeast; there is no third country-America or China or Myanmar making a claim over the northeast. This is a convenient point for the Government of India. These two cases are absolutely different. The only common thing is that they want to exercise their rights to self-determination as per the Article 1 of the International Covenant of Civil and Political Rights. Regarding the cease-fire in the northeast, as far as I understand, 2 section of the Naga movement is entering into ceasefire, they are supposed to have a political dialogue but in these four years, the dialogue has not given anything. No one known what's the outcome of four years dialogue.

At the same time another section of the Naga movement is not actively involved, though of the Government of India is persuading. In the northeast, the Naga factor is not complete. Half the Nagas are for ceasefire, half the Naga are not toeing the line. Then regarding all the other groups, they're not giving very good response. Whatever may be the nature of ceasefire, we cannot appreciate the position right now, unless they make out a case for themselves and the Government of India also comes out in no ambiguous terms about the holding of the political negotiation and about the demands made by the outfits.

***GO—What do you mean by right to self-determination? Does the right to secession form a* part of self determination?**

It was Niketa Krushchev of Soviet Union who said that colonised people should exercise their rights to self-determination. For that, full credit should be given to Krushchev, even though he was criticised as a revisionist. He made a big bang in the UN and 130 colonized people became independent and became members of the United Nations. Indian leader Nehru in 1937 also stood for decolonisation and he in his book, *The Discovery of India,* stood for the right to secession of legitimate states within India (p. 534). So far the definition of the right to self-determination is concerned there are two approaches.

One is a definition of self-determination according to the political need of a country. Secondly, a definition of self-determination by following International Covenant on Civil and Political Rights' (Article 1). So if we follow the convenient political' definition of self-determination of a country. Vajpayee (In case of Kashmir or the north east) or Putin (in case of Chechnya) or Chinese leadership (in case of Tibet) they may all have their own definition.

They don't want to include the territorial component in the exercise of the right to self-determination. This is very much disorganised and convenient method of defining self-determination. In India also, even in Assam, there are some scholars who define self-determination as autonomy or maximum autonomy. This is one process. But this is not a universally accepted definition within the State practice. This is a very ill-suited but politically convenient way of tackling their own national requirements and this does not meet with the universal benchmark of self-determination. Definition number two : Considering Article I of the Covenant 1966 and State practices and also decolonisation process under the auspices of the UN the right to self-determination does not pre-determine or assume anything till the concerned people exercise their rights fully.

Their should be a method, which is important. The people concerned should exercise their will either by plebiscite or referendum whether they want autonomy or want to form an Independent State including the territory. As in the case of East Timor, the United Nations had allowed (India supported that) that East Timorese people should exercise their right to self-determination.

In the exercise of self-determination, two options were given to them either autonomy within Indonesia, or opt for Independence. So, majority "opted for Independence. This *is* a State practice. So, according to the accepted State practises, as in the case of East Timor, Western Sahara, and elsewhere, the International Court of Justice had held that people themselves would decide their fate whether they want autonomy or total sovereignty. Therefore, right to self-determination is not closed thing it's an open-ended thing.

GO—Is it possible to assert a 'north-east identity' in the context of various 'homeland' demand, such as greater Nagaland, greater Assam, greater Mizoram etc.?

I can't appreciate the issue you've raised and the kind of problems all of us face in the region in defining northeast issues. That's true. But one thing is that by exercising the rule of exclusion. we've to exclude the provocative things like greater Assamese, greater Manipur, greater Mizoram and greater Nagaland issue. By doing so, we'll create permanent, damage to the peace and tranquility of the northeast. This is an impossible thing.

Look at the Palestinian issue. Palestinians had been rooted out of Israel in 1948 and they setlled in nearby five /six surrounding Arab countries and they're now trying to form a Palestinian State; with universal approval and tacit support from Israel. In the process the Palestinian leadership are wise that they did not demand amalgamation of Palestinian settled areas into Palestine. Otherwise, millions of Palestinians settled in the five or six major Arab contiguous areas, will be surrounded by hostile Arab States, which are otherwise friendly.

Similarly the world wherever there are international or national boundaries communities overlap the boundaries and if every country demanded that the overlapping population should be included with that country, then the world would be the unhapplest place to live in. It's impossible. If this argument is extended, then Tamil Eelam should be a part of Tamil Nadu or 'Tamil Nadu should be separated from India to Join the Tamil Eelam.

In the same vein of argument, Bangladesh and West Bengal will combine together as Bengalis overlap each other's boundary. It cannot be done it should not be done. It's morally an indefensible position. But may be in the colonial history, there were certain settled boundary that should be accepted. In the case of any conflict. The parties concerned should come to the negotiating table; they should bring out their historical records and settle it through a boundary commission and not by unilateral claims. It will be provocative.

GO—Isn't that what's happening in the Northeast with major people's groups asserting competing identities such as, Nagas, Mizos, Manipuri?

North-east is a plural concept with unity in attitude. But even then in political language the north-east is a federal concept. Without inter-dependence and mutual help, northeast is not a viable proposition. It's an impossible thing. So, claiming greater land greater things, is a contradiction to permanent peace in the northeast and no wise statesman could have ever made such a claim, except that when they so much internally weak. In order to organise themselves, they make hot slogans, just like the political parties in Delhi. They may do it, but it's not viable.

Besides, the international Court of Justice, State practices and International law always maintain that the colonial boundaries should be retained. If these colonial boundaries are disturbed, there may be war in the pre-colonial areas and the independence will have no meaning. I think wise statesmen will follow the International Court of Justice ruling in many cases.

Secondly, regarding the generic term, the valley people want to use the term. Manipuri, to comprehend their own cognate brothers in the hills -- North and South, but now there are political pulls and pressures from Mizoram and some part of Northern Manipur State. They were proud to be Identified as Manipuris not only the valley people but also the other tribal brothers, and when the right historical moment comes, they would become more proud. Ab the moment , large there are push and pulls, and therefore we use the term people of Manipur and not Manipuris so that people in the valley and hills can comprehend the idea. However, a day will come when they themselves will voluntarily identify themselves as proud Manipuris.

GO—In the northeast we find jungle warriors, not best doctors, best engineers, best professionals. Don't you think it is time people look for alternative approach to finding solutions to their problems?

Yes, many groups have been fighting for the last 50 years and as I said, military solution is absolutely counter-productive. You've rightly added a new point here why they (armed outfits) didn't build up human resource. For that, the north-eastern people themselves are accountable. They should also see that when all these inevitable things are happening, they develop work culture they develop harmonious relationship between all the communities, linguistic groups in the northeast. They'll have to develop that culture. Rule of exclusion is not always good. Some time it operates, often it does not work.

Every north-eastern or should see that the rule of exclusion should be used very rarely. Whenever there is a multi-linguistic group we should see that a common language is spoken. There are certain chauvinist elements in Assam. Manipur who always speak in terms of their own language. I also want a good language policy for the northeast. In regard to Manipur, I also strongly feel that the valley people the Meities, should also learn at least one tribal language. — Naga or Kuki language. Every mass gathering I address, I always insist on this point. One should not be proud of speaking only Meitei language, although, mother speaking tongue is sweet for all.

It's true that we should produce world-class doctors engineers, lawyers, and businessman. But, you must also accept that Manipur can produce world class Olympians. If Kunjarani were given a chance she would have brought a gold not the bronze and it celerbrated for many days for that.

Had Kunjarani been selected against Maleswari, every sports writer, both foreign and Indian media, predicted Kunjarani would have got gold. So that mistake was not Kunjarani, but of the Government of India. The Government of India was rather virtually racial they wanted a bronze brought by Maleswari rather than trying for gold from Kunjarani. We're producing world class people in the field of sports, culture, literature, among others.

Index

A

AFSPA, 96, 100-02, 105, 106, 108, 109, 111, 115, 121, 129, 131, 132, 141, 144, 148, 150, 178
AIDS, 101
Anti National Elements, 111
Arab countries, 247
Armed Forces [Special Powers) Act, 1958, 105
Army Corps, 115
Arunachal Pradesh, 134
Assam, 85, 95, 113, 134, 177, 250
Australoid groups, 243
Austric, 243

B

B.P. Jeevan Reddy, 104
British India, 113, 135, 242

C

Cambodia, 6
Central African Republic, 5
Centrality of National Question, 88
Churchill, 80
Civil and Political Rights, 246
Clash of Civilisations, 83, 86
COHR, 137
Cold War, 189
Committee on Human Rights, 137
Continuous crimes, 16
Criminals, 120

D

DICTUM, 190
Discovery of India, 246
Dominic Ongwen, 14
Downing Street declaration, 193
Dr. Krishnaswami, 110

E

East Timor, 8, 91, 244
economic globalization, 85
ECOSOC, 241
Embedded Political Immorality, 96

F

Federalism, 173

First World War, 83
FRETLIN, 194
Fukuyama, 83

G

Geneva, 191
  Conventions (1949), 8, 11, 98, 121
George Mitchell, 192, 193
Germany, 80
Globalization, 85
Goebbel, 150
GOI, 244
Gonds, 120
Good Friday Agreement, 192

H

Hague Invasion Act, 21
Hindusthani, 114
HIV, 101
Human rights, 97
  Commission, 102
  Covenants, 119
  in Armed Conflict Areas, 93
  Jurisprudence, 130
Humanitarian Laws, 116

I

ICC, 4, 5, 14, 16
  jurisdiction, 9
  jurisprudence, 18
  Rome treaty, 1998, 102
ICCPR, 97, 104, 119, 121, 136, 141, 145
ICTR, 4, 8, 9, 10
ICTY, 4, 8, 9, 10
IMT, 13
Indian,
  Federal Question, 175
  Independence Act, 1947, 187
Indigenous Peoples, 241
Individual criminal, 11
Indonesia, 8
Indo-Sri Lanka Agreement, 195
International
  Court, 3, 14
  Tribunal, 8
  Guarantor, 192
  Standard, 119
IPKF, 195
IRA leadership, 192
Iraq, 7
Ivica Rajic, 8

J

Jeevan Reddy Committee, 148
Jews, 80
Jokic, 8
Joseph Kony, 14
Jus Cogens, 131, 139
Justice Reddy Report, 104

K

Kuki language, 250
Kunjarani, 250

L

Labour Party, 193
Law and order, 120
Liberation wars, 90
Lord Linlithgow, 102
LRA, 14
LTTE, 195
Lubango Dyilo, 5

M

Mac Arthur, 12
Maleswari, 250
Manipur, 113, 134, 137, 242, 250
    Communist Party, 89
Martinovic, 8
Meghalaya, 134
MHA, 107
Militarization of civil society, 93
Mongolian people, 243

N

N. Sanajaoba, 240
Naga, 250
    hill, 89, 242
    movement, 245
Nagaland, 134, 242
Nalatilic, 8
NAM, 119
Namibia, 244
National Commission, 176
Nehru, 246
NGOs, 100
Nikolic, 8
NLM, 120
NSA, 5, 98
NSGT, 112, 114, 123, 126, 129, 139
NSL, 120

O

Okot Odhiambo, 14
OTP, 5, 15

P

Palestine, 190
Palestinian issue, 247
Peace Initiative, 80
PIB reports, 115
PLA, 4
POTA, 101
PUDR, 146
Puerto Rico, 244

Q

Quit India, 175

R

R. M. Pal, 12
Raska Lukwiya, 14
Revolutionary United Front, 6
Right to life, 141
Rome Treaty, 3
Roosevelt, 80

ROQUE, 119
RUF, 6
Rungsung Suisa, 109

S

Samuel Huntington, 83
Sarkaria Commission, 175
Second World War, 83
Sharm El Sheikh Agreement, 191
Sikkim, 174
Soviet Union, 91
Special Powers of Armed Forces, 108
Sri Lanka, 195
Sri Lankan army, 195
Sri Warior, 110
Stakic, 8
Stalin, 80
Sudan, 4
Supreme Court verdict, 135

T

TADA, 129
Tamil Eelam, 248
Tamil Nadu, 248
Thimpu principles, 195
Third Reich, 126, 137
Third World War, 83
Timor problem, 91
Tokyo tribunal, 12
Tripura, 113, 134, 242
Truth commissions, 18

U

Uganda, 5, 14
ULFA, 177
ULP, 117
  Act, 132
UNAMET, 194
UNHRC, 145
United Nations, 91
  Human Rights Committee, 133, 141
United States, 82
Unlawful Activities (Prevention) Act 1967, 120
UNMISET, 194
UPC, 4
USA, 119, 188, 190, 240

V

Venezuela, 15
Vietnam, 188
  War, 189
Vincent Otti, 14

W

Western Sahara, 244
WMD, 7
Wye II, 191

Y

Yandabo Treaty, 242
Yugoslavia, 8